Know Your Children in School

LUCY SPRAGUE MITCHELL

CLAUDIA LEWIS

VIRGINIA SCHONBORG

RUTH A. SONNEBORN

DOROTHY STALL

ILLUSTRATIONS BY ANNE HEYNEMAN

Bank Street College of Education

KNOW

YOUR

CHILDREN

IN

SCHOOL

The Macmillan Company
NEW YORK

L. F.

Contents

We want especially to express our thanks to the New York State Mental Health Authority whose generous grant has enabled us to make this volume available for all teachers seeking a fuller insight into the inner needs of children.

Know Your Children in School

About This Book

All the children in these sketches are real children. The stage-set in which we see these children is real. The problems we see them struggling with—sometimes with anxiety, sometimes with eagerness—are real. And real are the problems of the teachers who are trying to understand the new thinking that has entered the curriculum since they were trained how to teach, teachers who are trying to understand their children. Teachers, not only parents, call these school children "theirs." In so doing, they are recognizing that they as well as parents have a responsible and significant human relationship with the children in their classrooms. And real, too, very real are the problems of the many parents who are trying to understand "their" children at home. Parents and teachers are concerned for the same children, and what happens to the children at home and in school. That is why the Bank Street College of Education thinks these sketches of real children in real schools concern parents and teachers alike. Both groups are trying to know "their" children in school.

The word-sketches in this book are based on records made in the Bank Street Workshops in public schools in New York City. Records have been condensed and freely combined in some of the sketches. And they have been cast into dramatic form. But the remarks made by the children have not been invented, nor have the situations which evoked these remarks. These sketches are not intended to highlight any actual child, teacher or school, nor to illustrate problems and procedures which are relevant to New York City schools alone. In the aggregate, however, these glimpses of children and teachers in action together exemplify the kinds of situations that may arise in almost any classroom.

What are the Bank Street Workshops?

They are experiments in inservice education of teachers, sponsored since 1943 by the Board of Education of the City of New York. The Workshop program is carried out through two major and supplementary techniques: the first is group discussions with teachers who voluntarily join the Workshop; the second is work with these teachers on an individual basis. At weekly after-school meetings, the teachers bring up for discussion any problems about children and methods of meeting children's needs, about teaching techniques or programs and methods of building a curriculum. These discussions often lead to a request for more systemized talks by a Bank Street staff member or invited speakers. Through individual conferences with a Bank Street staff member and help in their classrooms, individual teachers have the chance to apply the more general thinking of the group discussions to their own particular children and their own backgrounds and ways of approaching children and their teaching job.

The first Bank Street Workshop began shortly before the New York City Board of Education issued a new curriculum Bulletin which differed importantly from the old curriculum in its approach to both children and subject matter. Fundamentally, the Workshop was designed to help teachers understand this new approach and to apply it in their own classrooms with efficiency and pleasure. The first Workshop staff was made up entirely of staff of the Bank Street College. Now the Board of Education has released from classrooms five of their teachers, former members of some of our Workshops, to become members of the Bank Street Workshop staff.

Why has the Bank Street College asked one-time members of the Workshop staff to write these sketches of some of the children they knew in school classrooms from kindergarten through sixth grade?

The answer lies chiefly in the desire to have the "new education" thought of not merely in the cold terms of theory based on scientific findings, but also in the warm terms of human situations where real children and real teachers live and learn together.

The writers of these sketches brought more than theory and scientific findings to the situations they describe. They all brought the experience of many years of teaching children, years of learning how to build a curriculum of experiences for children. More than that, they all brought a belief that children have greater potentialities for growth than are as yet being developed in their schools and homes, and a belief that through the development of children's potentialities lies the best chance for a better life for them as individuals and for the society of which they will be adult members. Above all, these writers brought a genuine love for children as human beings—immature but with personalities to be respected and developed.

To succeed, the new education must involve more than an intellectual approach. It must involve a feeling approach. Of course, we need the clearly defined analysis of what children are like, what they are interested in, what they need and how they learn. We need, too, curriculum guides for teachers set up within the framework of what children are like. But these formal statements alone do not stir and stimulate us as do visits to the classrooms where we see children and teachers in action together. Nor can word pictures stir and stimulate as do actual visits and direct observation. Yet these sketches, we hope, do let children themselves tell what they are like, and reveal the vitality of their response to certain kinds of experiences which are possible in schools. Also, we hope these sketches, though vicariously, will convey something of the pleasure, the satisfaction, yes, the excitement that we ourselves have experienced directly through knowing these children and teachers and many hundreds like them. We wish to share our experience with others. We hope that our experience, in some small way, may illuminate and deepen the significance of being a teacher of children today. And in addition we hope that teachers, parents and others too, will simply enjoy being with these children who must be like many they know. For all these reasons we are publishing these sketches of real children in real school situations.

The sketches in this book are about boys and girls. The boys in the sketches seem to cause their teachers more trouble than the girls—which probably reflects the real situation in many classrooms. How far the different behavior of boys and girls reflects different cultural pressures to which they have been subjected is an intriguing question that has never been satisfactorily explored, so far as we know. But we think it safe to say that trouble-makers are not the only children who have troubles, that girls have no fewer troubles, no less acute needs than boys.

The children in this book cover a wide age-range—from five-year-olds or a little younger who are having their first adventure in group life at school, through eleven- or twelve-year-olds who will soon leave the elementary school for junior high school. We are including such a wide age-range intentionally. Teachers and parents are coming to think of their children as in a *stage of development* and to recognize that at each stage children commonly show both lags from an earlier stage and hints of maturity that will come to fulfilment in a later stage. These sketches show children of the same age who are nevertheless in different stages of maturity—physical, mental, emotional and social maturity. Modern psychology teaches there is no hard and fast "norm" which all children should reach at a given chronological age. Nevertheless, there is a certain consistency about growth. Children pass through much the same stages of development but at their individual tempo and in their individual ways. Every teacher—and every parent who has more than one child—knows this, and it should no longer worry anyone. For the new thinking about children has brought new thinking about the role of the adults who are important in children's lives. That role is no longer to force their children to reach a definite norm in achievement and in behavior at a given age. Rather their role is to give their children the fullest possible opportunities to grow in healthy all-around ways and to be content if their children are growing. We believe the concepts of *growth* and of *maturity levels* (rather than age levels) are among the most significant in understanding human beings of any age from birth to death. These concepts lie behind the sketches in this book. We think these all-important concepts are clarified by seeing the sweep of children's growth as they successively develop new interests, new powers, new sensitivities on their march towards maturity. Every child brings his past with him and carries his present into the future. These sketches show the typical needs of children as

15

they grow up. They sometimes show what are the undeveloped potentialities of these children. They suggest attitudes towards these children and school experiences which may develop these potentialities. Taken together, they show how a school *may be a place for children to grow in*.

The first sketches in this book about five, six and seven-year-old children, written by a member of the faculty of Bank Street College, were published in 1946 by the Board of Education of New York City as a bulletin called: *Teacher! Are These Your Children?* This bulletin is now out of print. We wish to express our thanks to the Board for its cooperation and encouragement in the preparation not only of these first sketches, but also of the later sketches about children from seven-and-a-half years to twelve. None of the latter have appeared before in printed form. All are based on work in New York City public schools.

We owe thanks to many individuals in the New York schools who have supported our experiment in inservice education in our Bank Street Workshops—our district superintendents, principals of schools, teachers—many, many teachers. We do thank them all though their number is too great to name each one here. Special thanks are due to Regina C. M. Burke, formerly Associate Superintendent in charge of Elementary Schools, and William H. Bristow, Director, Bureau of Curriculum Research, for their cooperation as sponsors and consultants; and to Barbara Biber, Annette Frank, Mildred Greenwald, Vivienne Hochman, Ralphine Kessler, Tillie Pine, Charlotte Winsor, who as members of the Bank Street Workshop Staff, assisted in the collection and editing of this material.

LUCY SPRAGUE MITCHELL

By CLAUDIA LEWIS:

Prologue

Kindergarten, First, and Second Grade Children

The first day of school—"that most important, most beautiful first morning"—as a teacher herself described it, looking back on her own childhood.

From the door of home to the door of school—what momentous steps! They are taken, to be sure, in a mixture of "giant" and "baby" strides, and not without a looking backward to the well-known walls of home. But they mark a real transition. Though these young children will continue throughout their early school years to need and want their parents' love and protection as much as they ever did, it will be in a new way. Gradually they will begin to disdain the running to adult arms for comfort when things go wrong. They will not want to tell the adults around them all their secrets. More and more the group of peers will become the testing ground for social values, for belief in self. And more and more the search for heroes will open up new paths to follow, leading far afield.

The child in his first years of school—kindergarten,

first and second grades—has stepped out to meet the world, and to learn where he stands in it. He looks around at the other children who become his daily companions at school and wonders: Who are they? How do they act? Can he take a place among them? What do they love? What do they hate? How can he bind himself to them? He experiments with social interchange, just as he tests himself with balls and bats, books and pens; and he fumbles at first, and makes false moves in his inexperience. It will take him years of practice to find his skill.

He comes with active feet, investigating hands. In these early years it is the concrete world around him that challenges him—the noisy, moving world of things that he can see and hear and touch. Only later on, with his growing powers of conceptualization, will his curiosities carry him into explorations of the abstract world, the distant universe, the historical past.

At five or six, every hallway, every street, every passing train or truck lures him. "How does it work? Where does it go? Where did it come from?" These are his insistent questions. The wonderful workings of machines and engines and wheels, the ways of things that move above ground and under ground—from planes to subways, from clouds to rivers—he must find out about them all, touching, handling, watching.

And the mysterious symbols he sees about him—the words, the letters, the numbers, on signs along the street, in stores, on clocks—these, too, are a part of his immediate world. He wonders about their meanings, takes his first steps in mastering their use. At six he learns to tell the time, as at ten he will learn to trace the course of planets.

Here he stands at the schoolhouse door on this first day—curious, eager, excited, perhaps a little frightened, but ripe for growth and learning.

The schoolroom that he enters today is not like the schoolrooms of the old days. No longer is the teacher's job merely that of drilling her children in the 3 R's and keeping her class in order—if one may use the word "merely" in this connection. Perhaps it is unfair to do so. Teaching has never been easy, under any circumstances. Always it has demanded energy and patience and skill. And the best teachers, at all times, have felt just as responsible for helping their children to learn acceptable ways of behavior as for teaching them reading, writing, and arithmetic. The best teachers, at all times, have devoted themselves to the welfare of their children, and this has meant an unselfish and often exhausting giving of time and effort and interest.

Today, however, there are many ideas afloat concerning what constitutes the acceptable behavior and welfare of young children in school. Teachers know that they must now look beyond the schoolroom. There must no longer be any separation between behavior in school and behavior out of school. Teachers—especially teachers of the youngest children—are asked to make the schoolrooms homelike places where the boys and girls may move about and communicate with each other, and work and play actively. Teachers are asked to know and understand each child as never before, to help each child grow in the way that is best for him. The all-round development of children has become the educational goal.

If teaching in the past made great demands, today it seems to many teachers an almost overwhelming job. Kindergarten, first and second grade teachers are asking themselves questions like these:

How do I control children when I let them move around freely?

How much noise should I allow, and why?

Why are some of the children so rebellious, while others behave so well?

There are so many kinds of children to try to understand—the child who doesn't concentrate, the child who doesn't get along with others, the aggressive child. How can I learn to understand them all?

We try to build our curriculums around children's true interests and needs, but how can I be sure that I know what these needs are?

Here in these sketches are presented some of the problems that teachers are facing in the early grades—and some of the possible solutions.

These solutions are not offered in the form of neat little pills, however, applicable to all cases, because there are none such known in the realm of human behavior. They are to be thought of, rather, as stemming from and dependent upon certain attitudes—attitudes toward children and toward classroom curriculums and procedures. A teacher who adopts these attitudes can find her own solutions without too much difficulty, and she need not be magician, genius, psychiatrist. Teachers have done it, and they know they are successful when their children come up to them to tell them, as one of the children in these sketches really did: "I love school. It's just like home."

KINDERGARTEN
SCENES

¶ ALLEN, The Disturber

Allen has not been in kindergarten very long—he entered late in the spring—and every day since his arrival he has stuck out like a sore thumb. Trouble, trouble, his middle name is trouble.

Any teacher knows how it is. When all the rest of the children are quietly drinking milk, he will suddenly burst out with loud caw-caw sounds.

He invariably needs to go out to the bathroom at irregular times, and when he opens the door and returns from one of these trips, he comes in with great stamps of the feet and shouting of nonsense, distracting everyone's attention from the story that is being read.

If he can be persuaded to sit with the others and listen to a story for a while, as likely as not he will suddenly

jump up in the midst of it and give the piano a bang, or start galloping off around the room.

When a flower is passed around for all of the children to smell, of course it is Allen who takes the opportunity to grab it, time and again.

He'll even slip out of the door sometimes and run away down the hall, against all the rules.

Mischief, mischief, and trouble, trouble.

Look at him now. His teacher has just tacked up on the bulletin board a beautiful new picture of a pig, and has been talking with the children about it. They are getting busy with their crayons and paper, to draw some animals. But not Allen. What new deviltry is he up to? He is approaching the pig picture, crayon in hand. Is he actually going to scribble on it? Look, he has made a tiny green mark on the picture. But—he is keeping his eye on the teacher. He turns, he wants her to see him. He is holding his arm and hand up as though he were about to scribble all over the picture, but actually he is not doing anything to spoil it. He waits, he wants her to look, to see him doing this naughty thing. His whole expression shows that he is *pretending* to scribble, so that she will come rushing over to stop him.

She sees him out of the corner of her eye, but turns her back and avoids looking at him. Finally he gives up and goes to his table to draw pictures with the other children.

Ah, he has given himself away in this little incident.

Not Really Bad

He is not so much interested in doing "bad" things as he is in having her *see* him do them. In fact, he is not really a "*bad*" child. What a sense of right and wrong he really has, what self-control. He did not allow himself actually to destroy that nice picture.

No doubt all of his noise-making and disturbing are aimed, in just this way, directly at her.

But why is it so important to him that she see him doing these trouble-making things? Is it just that he wants "attention"? Before we can answer this we must know more about him.

His teacher tells us that Allen's father is away in the Army and that his mother has gone to work since Allen started coming to kindergarten. She turns him over to a neighbor woman and sees him herself only in the evenings.

Indeed, it is easy to believe that at home he may get very little "attention"—meaning that steady flow of parental affection, interest, and concern which every child should have as his birthright.

"Even so," you say, "why does he have to do all these naughty things to try to get the adult attention he needs? He'd make the adults feel much more kindly disposed toward him if he'd behave himself."

Well, here we need to look still further into the picture of his home life.

He Can't Help Himself

His mother's statement on the day she brought him to school to enroll him is very revealing:

"I don't care how much you beat him, just so there's breath left in his body . . . I just want to get rid of him a couple of hours, so I can have a little peace . . ."

And her behavior that afternoon when she called for him completes the picture. While she was helping him with his coat, she boxed him roughly around for no apparent reason except her own irritation.

Clearly, this suggests a home that is far from peaceful or happy, that has little love or warmth in it, that is filled with beatings and trouble.

23

Isn't it likely that Allen knows no way to get his mother interested in him except by cutting up and annoying her?

Doesn't it seem likely that his idea of an adult is someone who punishes?

And would it be hard to believe that this little boy may be driven, quite involuntarily, by a fierce need to rebel and do naughty things, perhaps in retaliation for his rough treatment, or to prove that he has some self-assertion left? (You know how it is. Punishment is pretty hard to take lying down. Let someone make a cutting or derogatory remark to us and even if we deserve it, it seems to force us to flare right up in self-defense.)

What To Do?

What should and can be done to help this little boy in school? What is his teacher's method of dealing with him? Does she punish him? Isolate him? Does he irritate her and make her cross?

We have already had a short glimpse of her in the act of purposely ignoring one of his attempts to annoy her. This might well lead us to believe that she is trying to show him he need not do naughty things in order to make her pay attention to him. Perhaps she is trying to teach him that there are other, more legitimate ways.

Look at her now. She is standing by his chair, watching him draw, and is telling him in an affectionate way what a fine picture he is making. In reality, it seems to be a rather poor drawing, compared with those the other children are making, but Allen has been working at it as well as he seems capable of working these days, and the praise may be just what he needs.

Yes, he looks up, beaming, and then gets right to work again, with even better concentration. Soon he has finished and looks up with a satisfied smile.

And what is his teacher doing now? She has opened her purse and has taken out a dollar bill. "Allen, you've been working so hard that I think you might enjoy going on a special little errand for me. Would you like to take this down the hall to Miss Smith's room? Tell her this is the money we owe her for the party."

Off he goes, eagerly. Can this child, who runs away, be trusted with a dollar bill? We'll see. It is very likely no one at home has ever given him any responsibilities. For all we know, he may rise to meet them as well as any child would, if not better. And the opportunity to go off down the hall for a legitimate and important reason may cure him of his desire to run away down this same hall.

Here he comes, back already, with a thank you note from Miss Smith. Meanwhile the other children have put away their crayons and are sitting quietly at the tables for their rest. Does Allen bang the door, or sing out loudly to annoy?

No, this time he comes in looking very self-possessed, and walks straight to his chair in a controlled and businesslike manner. Apparently the errand *has* done something for him. It has made him feel important and good in his teacher's eyes. There is no need for him to bang the door this time, to attract her attention to him.

He Doesn't Need Punishment

Clearly, this teacher realizes that no amount of punishing or lecturing to Allen can produce the desired results. Punishment is all he's had at home.

But even a small amount of affection and of praise (whenever it can be given for the slightest little thing he does well) may work a metamorphosis in time.

Allen has a lot to learn, of course, more than can be learned in just a few days. But let him gradually find that it is not necessary to be bad to make an adult interest herself in him, and let him learn, especially, that there are adults in the world who *like* him and whose affection and fairness and understanding he can count on. This can be his kindergarten lesson for the whole year, and if he learns these things and nothing else whatever, then kindergarten has been an invaluable experience for him and may make all the difference in the kind of school career that lies ahead of him in the grades.

¶ FREDDIE, Who Cannot Concentrate

Here is another little boy who is new in the kindergarten, and a puzzler he is.

One begins to wonder—is the child in a daze all the time? Is he a little slow at understanding? Something wrong with his intelligence?

He never seems to concentrate on any one thing, never finishes what he starts, rarely pays attention to what the other children are doing, and is all over the place, darting from one thing to another.

During the reading of a story he appears to be a thousand miles away. And he'll never sit through a whole story without getting up a hundred times to change his place. Obviously, he's not listening to the story.

During the singing his attention is all on what another child is doing at the other end of the room.

If he comes up and asks for help with the buckle of his snowsuit, he'll wander off while his teacher is in the very midst of helping him, because his eye has lighted on a toy train across the room.

If the children are all invited to come and see Henry's fine blockbuilding, Freddie may or may not come. If he does, he'll be off in just a minute to start wheeling the doll carriage around—and just as impulsively and unreasonably he'll suddenly leave that and turn to something else.

During rhythms when the game is played of marching and stopping exactly when the music stops, he alone does not heed the stopping places, but marches dazedly on, intent upon his own purposes.

What is the matter with this little boy? And what should his bewildered teacher do to help him settle down? Isn't he just wasting his time?

But wait, where is he now? For the last ten minutes he has been contentedly occupied at something, and has actually *not* been streaking around the room like a waterbug. He is in the little "playhouse"—the three-sided, roofless playhouse in the corner of the room. We can peek over the wall and see what he is doing inside.

There he sits by the little ironing board. Gently and carefully he "irons" a large piece of blue cloth, folding it, turning it, ironing and ironing away with great calmness and concentration. Can this be Freddie?

A little girl sits near him, carrying on a telephone conversation with the toy telephone. Soon she leaves the playhouse, and Freddie is alone there with just one other child, who busies himself "cooking dinner." Freddie irons and irons.

So! He *can* concentrate. What is there about this ironing that has done the trick?

There Must Be a Reason

Possibly this child has been somewhat overwhelmed by all the wealth of new things that have confronted

him upon his entry into the kindergarten. Not only is the room a very large one, no doubt five or six times larger than any room at his home, but it is filled with things he may never have seen before—easels, little tables and chairs, shelves full of games, toys, blocks. And think of the number of children! Now, within the little playhouse, his range is restricted. There are neither so many things nor so many children to distract him, and here in this comfortable little enclosure he can settle down.

Possibly no one has ever read stories to him before, and he scarcely knows how to sit and listen to one. Possibly no one has ever tried to teach him a song, or a game of marching and stopping. These are strange new experiences. But ironing—this is like home, something he knows about and understands.

It may very well be that he is a somewhat less mature child, emotionally and socially, than most of the others, and so finds it harder to adjust to the new school life, harder to depart from the familiar things of home.

Possibly too, concentration on "school" things comes hard for this little boy right now. We know something about his troubled, broken-up home life (mother and father recently separated), about the threats with which he is delivered at school. "If you aren't good you'll have to go to bed as soon as you come home."

All of us know our own personal troubles can play havoc with our concentration on our work.

So, whether it is the bewildering newness of school or the urgency of his own problems, or both, that are bothering Freddie, possibly this quiet little playhouse corner, secluded and comfortable, with the familiar ironing board in it, gives him more feeling of ease, more opportunity to concentrate than he can have anywhere else in the room, or in any other situation.

These, of course, are only "possibly's." The best we can do is watch Freddie and attempt to understand him, patiently trying one thing after another until we find what seems to be the right answer for him, the right activity and handling that will help him begin to settle down and feel at home in this schoolroom.

—Remembering, of course, that for another child, ironing in the playhouse may not be the solution at all.

¶ CHRISTINA, Who Never Causes Any Trouble

Who is the little girl who never has to be reminded that she is getting too noisy?—Christina.

Who never causes any trouble in the classroom? Never bothers anyone, never quarrels, never does what she is not supposed to do?—Christina.

A teacher's joy.

But is she, really? Should she be?

A teacher is scarcely apt to notice a little girl like this, who creeps so mouse-like through the day. The boisterous, noisy, rebellious children are the ones who force the teacher to watch them and do something about them.

But we, who have the privilege of looking into these classrooms without any of the responsibilities of managing them, can concentrate on Christina for a while and watch her in her kindergarten room.

There she sits, along with three others, at the table where the crayons are. What a solemn little face! Does she never smile? And isn't she going to join in any of the conversation? The other three are chatting quietly and happily. Why, Christina seems not to be a part of this group at all. Not a word does she speak during this whole half hour. And what is she drawing? Only a few tentative, timid little lines on her paper. Most of the time she seems to sit there, absently, just staring at the other three, who pay no attention to her.

Maybe later on she will talk and smile. But watch her during rhythms. She wears that same solemn little face. She goes through the rhythms in an automatic way, almost as though attached to the others by a string and therefore obliged to do what they do, but without volition or any animation on her own part. And still not a word does she speak.

When the teacher reads a story to the children, Christina sits with the group, but never does she chime in or pipe up as the others do. She wears that same solemn, absent little expression.

When it is time to get coats on and go home at 3 o'clock, Christina is one of the first to have her coat on and slip into her chair to wait for the dismissal signal from the teacher. There she sits, serious, quiet, "good," –hands folded.

Not Even a Mouse

Suddenly there is a commotion at the front of the room. A mouse in the cupboard! Most of the children rush up to peek in. But Christina? No, she sits there like a part of the furniture, and nothing will move her but the teacher's dismissal signal.

That child has not spoken one word to anyone in these two hours, nor has she shown any real spark of interest in the activities in this room. She does what she is supposed to do, down to the nth degree—follows all the rules, obeys the teacher, but otherwise she might just as well not be in the room.

We could well formulate a new set of questions about this little girl:

Who is the child who needs a good deal of help in making social contacts with the other children?—Christina.

Who is the child who may be "good" partly because of undue timidity?—Christina.

Who is the child who may be so troubled by the emotional problems she brings to school with her from home that she will need very special attention before she is at ease in this classroom?—Christina.

Who is the subdued little child in the room who may in reality be a more seriously maladjusted child than any of the lively disobedient ones?—Christina.

The Real Problem

The obstreperous children are classroom problems, no doubt about it. The teacher cannot let them upset the class and run wild.

But here is a plea for the forgotten Christinas, the mousy, quiet, conforming little children. More often than not, they are the ones who may present social and emotional maladjustments of a really deep-seated nature. The psychologists tell us this, over and over again. It is not Johnny, who dashes so wildly and noisily up to see the mouse, whose activity should worry us. It is rather Christina who should concern us, Christina who holds back and is too timid or too afraid of mixing with the others, or too dependent on teacher for her every move, or too absorbed in troubles to care about dashing up there.

Johnny is showing normal lively curiosity, and if he does upset a few rules sometimes he is not to be blamed for his strong independent urges. Rather, we should be glad he has them, and help him use them in constructive directions.

It is the shy, meek child, *unable* or *afraid* to show any normal rebellion or initiative, who may fail to develop independence and self-reliance as he grows up. It is the too good child, over-dependent on teacher's approval, who may have an extremely hard time getting along with other children, and indeed may fail to meet the social requirements of his companions throughout life. It is the quiet little day-dreaming child—no disciplinary problem to anyone—who yet may be a very unhappy child, beset with all sorts of inner troubles. Such a child's "good" behavior, as in Christina's case, is only a mechanical sort of thing, without a basis in good adjustment.

Watch Christina and the others like her. Get acquainted with them! They may need our help urgently in a good many different directions—and if we cannot get at the bottom of their behavior, then we may need to summon social worker, psychologist, or psychiatrist.

¶ JIMMY AND MARTIN,
Who Lost An Opportunity

The setting is the schoolroom, early in the afternoon.
Some of the children are sitting at the tables working
with clay. Others are coloring pictures for their writing
books. Jimmy is down on the floor in the corner where
the blocks are, building away.

Jimmy appears to be working hard on an idea. See
that serious thinking-frown on his face. "No, the blocks
don't go *this* way but *that* way," he seems to say. He
takes down one part of his building and tries it over
again. He is probably making the stable the children
went to see last week.

Suddenly Martin swoops down on the floor and joins
Jimmy.

Who is Martin?—That appealing but troubling little
boy who can't seem to learn to read or write; who never
stays at one thing more than a few minutes; who wants
a lot of teacher's attention; who demands special privi-
leges; who never will join in the things all the rest of the
children are doing unless he can have a special part
created more or less for him. Martin, the problem child,
the trouble-maker.

Trouble Ahead

What's he up to, down here on the floor with Jimmy?
Like a little eel he has suddenly started to wriggle through

33

the large archway that Jimmy must have intended as the entrance to the stable.

Crash! Of course. But since the blocks all fall on Martin, it's a rather silent crash, and the teacher doesn't happen to notice.

Martin extricates himself and sits up in the midst of the destruction he has wrought.

He glances at Jimmy. And what's in that glance? Martin could not say it in so many words, but the meaning is there:

"Well, well, how did that happen!"

And probably deep within, he is unconsciously feeling:

"I can't let you get away with being the boy who builds a fine stable that everyone will praise!"

And what about Jimmy! He has a glance too, a glance of utter dismay, questioning, distress.

But does he say anything to Martin? Does he demand help on rebuilding? Does he push Martin away in honest anger? Does he say even so much as "leave me alone, you bad boy"? Not a word.

Instead, he turns and looks toward the teacher, and in that look we can read a whole history:

"Teacher, Martin isn't fair. He ought not do this. Won't you please see what he's done, and do something about it? This is the schoolroom and I don't dare hit him or yell at him and create a scene. It's just impossible to do anything like that in school. I've got to be a good quiet boy and keep your approval, so I won't make any trouble, but please, please, teacher, look and see what he has done!"

Unfortunately, teacher doesn't happen to look this time, because she is so busy with her big roomful of children.

Martin darts away, and as he passes Elsie he rips a piece out of her clay bird nest. He knows she won't raise any protest.

And Jimmy? Well, Jimmy just decides he might as well give up. He gets up, leaving his blocks in a heap, and wanders over to get some clay.

What Price "Order?"

It isn't the teacher's fault for not happening to see that little episode, of course. No teacher in a roomful of 30 or 35 active children can possibly see everything that happens to every child, all the time.

But what a loss!—Jimmy's building in ruins, and all that constructive thinking and planning cut short; Jimmy's sense of righteousness outraged, and an attitude of meek non-protest encouraged; and another victory chalked up for Lord Martin, who knows he can trample all over the other children when teacher isn't looking. That is, it is another "victory" from his standpoint, but from ours it is another defeat, carrying him further and further away from a happy relationship with the other children and a happy adjustment to himself.

What would have happened if Jimmy had felt free to protest vigorously to Martin? If his teacher had taught him to try to deal directly with the child who bothers him, rather than always waiting for her to step in? (This does not necessarily mean that he should have

35

started a real fight in the schoolroom. It might mean that he could have run after Martin and insisted on help in rebuilding the stable, or at least in piling up the blocks.)

What if all the other Jimmys and Elsies in the room felt perfectly free to stand up for their rights—*even if it meant making a little noise and rumpus?*

In the long run it would probably be a big help to Martin, and obviously he is a child who needs help, all that he can get. He might really "come around" if he perceived that the *other children*, as well as the teacher, were going to set limits on his behavior, and would not tolerate being walked all over.

Wouldn't it do something for Jimmy and Elsie too? Do we really want to foster an attitude of meek, helpless acceptance of injustice? Do we want the children to be so dependent on us to straighten out their troubles? Is this training in democratic living? And do we really value a quiet and orderly room at such a cost?

Just what is this "school behavior" we expect of our children?

Does it bear any relation to real life behavior?

Where does the concept come from?

¶ EUGENE, So Sullen!

His teacher has despaired of doing very much to help him. Day after day he is the same—sulky, moody, cross. He mopes off by himself, with an unhappy look. Almost any little thing seems to bring this mood upon him. Ask him to share the paste with the boy next to him, and there comes that irritable frown on his face. The next moment he may have his head down on the desk, weeping silent aggrieved tears. And then suddenly he begins vindictively grabbing at all his belongings, as though every child were against him and about to snatch things from him.

He never says very much, and it's hard to figure out what's bothering him so. The other children are really very nice to him and like him, but day after day he's the same, his face black with frowns.

"And what can I do to help him?" his teacher says.

"More Than I Can Handle"

"Probably it's his home situation to blame, and what headway can I make against that? I know he's come up recently from a little country place in the South, and his family is all broken up—his mother is working all day now, and a grandmother has appeared on the scene to help care for the children. All these changes may have been pretty hard on him, but they're out of my control. I really think a lot of these problem children come to us with problems bigger than we can handle . . .

"Of course, there are some things Eugene likes to do in school, such as a dramatic train game we play, and I give him a chance to be in the game as often as possible, since it does help to brighten him up, but this is only a drop in the bucket, so it seems. Ten minutes later he may turn sullen again."

Let's open the door and take a look at this unhappy boy in action.

His class has just returned from a walk to the river. It is a warm morning. The children all look very relaxed and ready to rest after their exertion.

In fact, there is Eugene already resting. He is sitting at his seat with his head down on the desk. Or maybe he is crying? His teacher speaks to him and he does not respond. Why, he is *sleeping*—no doubt about it.

"This has never happened in school before!" his teacher exclaims. "I suppose the warmth of the day explains it, and all of the exercise. Yet, none of the other children have fallen asleep . . .

"This makes me wonder if some of his sullen, frowning expression has been due to nothing but pure and simple tiredness. It's quite likely that he gets to bed very late, in that crowded little flat, and I know he does not have a bed to himself . . .

"Possibly, if I could somehow arrange for him to have a real rest in school . . . Or if the social worker could help on this problem . . ."

Not So Complicated

This teacher is on the right track.

It's far too early to give up hope of helping a child on his "emotional" problems until all the possibilities of interpreting them at least partly as *physical* problems have been exhausted.

Of course, in Eugene's case, the problems probably do extend out of the purely physical realm into the complexities and difficulties of the upset home. His teacher cannot afford for a minute to stop searching into *all* the causes of his sullenness and attempting in every way she can think of to make things happier for him. She has already made a fine beginning by drawing Eugene frequently into the train game he likes so well, and she should not feel that this is a hopelessly insignificant drop

in the bucket. Not only does she give him the pleasure of the game, but by letting him play it often she undoubtedly is giving him some feeling of her friendly concern for him.

No doubt Eugene will continue to need this friendly assurance, even if some provision is made for him to get extra rest and sleep.

But the important point is this: Who can say that Eugene's "emotional" problems may not appear much less formidable after all the *physical* ones are taken care of? We do not know for sure that Eugene's moody frowns are due partly to lack of sleep, but it seems very likely. By all means, let his teacher take hope.

The physical problems usually can be coped with much more easily than the emotional. And how often they are overlooked!

¶ MICHAEL, So Lively!

His teacher complains that she just can't keep him down. He can't stop talking or sit still, always wants a turn at everything, dashes around the classroom. In fact, he's always so much in the foreground, piping up, doing this and that, that sometimes she's hardly aware of the other children in the room at all. She's always having to speak to Michael, send him back to his seat, or tell him he has to let the others have turns, though he is agreeable enough and seems to mean well.

Let's see what she means. Let's look in on Michael in his first grade room on several different days, in several different situations.

1

It is springtime, and the children are planting some bulbs. The teacher has placed a table in the front of the

39

room. One at a time a few of the children are called upon to come up and put a bulb in a pot, or pour on some water. Most of the children stay in their seats to watch this activity, craning their necks, to be sure, but remaining seated until called upon. Not so Michael— little sparkling-eyed, quick-moving fellow. He keeps dashing up to the front to take a close look at a bulb just planted, or at a new handful of bulbs the teacher has just brought out. Repeatedly she sends him back. He never makes any real trouble about this and does dash back to his seat each time just as quickly as he left it, as though he had not really meant to fail to cooperate with the teacher—as though, in fact, he scarcely realized that he had done anything he was not supposed to do. He is obviously tremendously interested in all this planting activity, and seems to be pulled up there to the front of the room irresistibly, as though by a magnet. He keeps up a steady running commentary of talk, too, with such explosions as: "*That* isn't enough water! Put on more!" The things he says seem to be such a natural expression of his interest in the planting that one wonders not why he talks so much, but how the others can possibly keep so still.

2

The children are just leaving the classroom to go down to recess. Michael is lagging at the end of the line—but "lagging" is scarcely the word for it. He has a definite reason, apparently, for remaining at the end. When almost all of the children are out of the room he begins to whirl around up there in the front of the classroom where there is quite a lot of floor space. He seems to be practicing a special kind of whirl—on one foot, swinging himself around with a quick arm movement. Is he a baseball player? Is he the propellor of an airplane? How skillfully he zooms around! It is beautiful to watch. But now he dashes out of the room to catch up with the rest of the class. For half the way down the hall he remains at the end of the line, doing his whirl, apparently completely oblivious of the fact that he is supposed to be quietly walking and *not* whirling.

"Michael, Michael—at it again! Come up here and walk with me," his teacher calls when she looks around and sees him.

Just as quickly as he began his whirls, Michael snaps out of them, and trots up to the teacher, all willingness and co-operation.

3

It is very hard to manage an activity period in this room crowded with desks, but the teacher is courageously attempting it anyway. The children have been trying to construct some "properties" so that they can give a kind of play based on their study of the post-office in their neighborhood. Only a few children at a time can work on these things, but they have managed to make a "post-office" out of orange crates, there in the back of the room, and now a "mail truck" seems to be under construction. Michael stands beside an orange crate, holding the hammer. There is a little trouble, apparently, about whose turn it is to use the hammer. The teacher is asking Michael to let Clinton have a turn.

"O.K., he can have a turn pretty soon, but gee, I brought the box and I know how I want to make it. Just let me take this piece off and start it, or he won't get it right—"

Michael gets to work, and what a worker he is, skillful with the hammer, absorbed in his task. He does let Clinton have a turn, but in the end it is Michael who has done most of the work, and excellent work it is. He has a very ingenious idea about making a door on the end of the truck, and works away with concentration and energy as though his life depended upon it. One cannot blame him for his eagerness to "have the turn." He is bursting to see if he can give his good idea concrete shape.

4

Dismissal time. The teacher, who is standing near the door, has asked Michael to go and get her purse and keys from her desk. Delighted at this chance to move around, he starts right up to the desk. But is it a boy or an airplane, a boat, approaching? He holds his hands pointed in front of him, and steers his way along the aisles, making little motor-like put-put-put sounds.

"Michael! Do you have to make that noise?" his teacher calls.

Michael reaches the desk, drops his pointed hands, and turns into a little boy again. He finds the purse and keys and takes them over to the teacher, with little boy steps.

What is the trouble with Michael?

The only trouble in the whole wide world is that he

is a lively, intelligent, imaginative, well-adjusted boy trying his best to get along in a school room that has not yet been able to make the best provision for him, for all its many excellent beginnings.

"Trouble?"

Michael is probably as "normal" a child as we could hope to find in any school. He comes from a happy home, where he is well cared for and loved. He is strong and well developed physically. He has a keen curiosity and interest in the world around him. He is friendly, happy, and well liked by both children and adults. His inability to keep still does not at all indicate that he is trying to be a trouble to his teacher, trying to defy her. In fact, he is as pleasant a child to handle as any in the class. The teacher herself has explained this—"He's willing enough, so it seems, but just can't stay put in his seat, or stop talking."

Michael could be the very child the educators had in mind when they planned the active kind of program for the schools—Michael, the normal, happy, eager, lively boy.

More Power To Him!

Take that urge of his to be up there watching every bit of the bulb planting, to be up there making his own comment on every phase of it. What is this but that wonderful thing called "intellectual curiosity"? What is it but that much-to-be-valued urge to find out things for oneself, to inspect things at first hand, using one's own eyes and ears?

Take Michael's eagerness to do *all* the hammering on the mail truck. This can hardly be called selfishness. It is, rather, excitement over making and figuring out and doing. It is the very thing we should want to encourage in our children—the ability and the urge to put ideas into action. For indeed, a young child has only half

43

learned a thing if he has not had the opportunity to test and digest his learning in a concrete way. Take this matter of learning about a mail truck, for instance. A child does not really absorb all there is to learn about one by merely seeing one once. He really begins to learn when he attempts to construct one, and finds himself bumping up against all sorts of questions and difficulties that he must solve. "What did the writing on the truck say? Were there one or two doors? Are they kept locked, and how? I forgot to notice these things. I'll have to take another careful look."

If Michael were *not* filled with this impatient eagerness to try to make the mail truck in the way he thinks it should be, then we certainly should have cause for worry. The only "trouble" in connection with this hammering incident is not Michael's attitude, not his curiosity and his imagination, but the fact that there are not sufficient materials in the room to keep each child busy.

Take all this physical activity of Michael's, his whirling, his zooming up and down the aisles like a boat or plane. We can't label this "cutting up." This is not only the strong natural muscular urge of a healthy child to keep moving, but it is also a wonderful example of what is meant when the educators say that young children *think* with their whole bodies. They *become* boats, airplanes, propellers, when they are talking or thinking about them. This is what they mean when they say that play—imaginative dramatic play—is the child's own special technique, and that we will turn it into a valuable tool for learning if we know what we are about.

Just How Do We Do It?

Let's lift Michael up bodily out of his present classroom and put him down in an imaginary one—an ideal one, though not out of the realm of possibility, a classroom planned to meet every need of normal, active, alert children like himself. What would it be like?

Here is the room, large and light, equipped with movable tables and chairs. Everywhere are signs of constructive activity. There are several easels in the room, there are shelves and shelves of blocks. There are plants, animals, and a corner set up with electric plates for cooking. At one end of the room is a well-equipped carpenter shop, at the other a library. On the walls hang not only the children's own bright paintings, for decoration, but reading charts printed by the teacher, charts telling of all the interesting things the children are doing.

But the room is empty just now. Where are they?

Here they are, out on the sidewalk in front of the school, watching a steam roller patch up the street. Their teacher noticed them craning their necks from the window, so took them right out where they could have a better view and really see how the whole thing works. The children are frequently out on trips of this sort in their neighborhood, trips that give them the chance to find out more about the things in which they are interested, that give them the chance to explore, to raise questions, and to track down the answers in a first-hand way—that is, by using the convincing evidence provided by their own eyes, ears, and hands. Here in this class Michael's "intellectual curiosity" is stimulated at every turn—and satisfied—and stimulated again. The teacher watches his interests, his questions, and sees to it that they are kept alive. She doesn't let them die out for lack of fuel.

"How do those wiggly lines get stamped onto envelopes?" We'll go to the post-office to see.

"How do ferry boats go through the water if they are round at the ends and not pointed? *Do* they have points underneath?" We'll have to go to the dock and take a good look at one and see.

"Where does the truck take all the ashes it collects from the cans in front of our school?" We'll go and find out.

"How much water should bulbs have, anyway?" We'll let each child have his own bulb to plant and care for and experiment with.

Cooperation Too

And here, in this imaginary classroom, Michael has all the opportunity he could possibly want for trying to make things as he thinks they should go. See him hammering away here on his mail truck, figuring out how to make its door open like the real one. He has no need to let Clinton have a turn on this piece of work. Clinton is busy on something of his own. This doesn't mean that Michael never has to share and cooperate with others in this classroom. There are many opportunities for cooperative work and play. Watch him down on the floor with the others, helping to reconstruct the school neighborhood in the form of a "map" of blocks, all laid out with streets and buildings, and with strips of oilcloth for the rivers. Listen to these children planning and thinking and criticizing together. This is a form of "dramatic play"—play turned into a tool for learning:

MICHAEL: Look, Walter, you made the George Washington Bridge over the *Harlem* River instead of over the Hudson River. Don't you know the bridge over the Harlem River is a drawbridge?

MARY (chiming in): And anyway, if it is the George Washington Bridge, it's not high enough. My boat can't go under it and all boats have to be able to go under the George Washington Bridge.
(In the midst of this conversation there is a sudden collision of boats in the middle of the river, boats carefully built up of blocks and pushed around on flat boards.)

JAMES: Look, teacher, La Verne just came bumping along with her boat and knocked mine all to pieces.

TEACHER: Well, James and La Verne, this reminds me. Boats have regular signals they use when they pass each other, so they know what side to pass on. When we take our trip to the river tomorrow, we'd better listen to these signals and try to learn something about them. Then we won't have so much trouble. And if we can't find out that way, maybe we can write to the Port Authority.

Nor is this play with the block "map" of the city the only kind of cooperative dramatic play that goes on in this room. Here Michael can "be" a boat or a plane to his heart's content—and much to his advantage from an educational standpoint.

It's More Than "Just Play"

The whole class is having a rhythms period. It is fine exercise, but far more. Here, too, the teacher has turned this play technique into a tool for learning.

A group of eight children are in what they call a "ferry boat" formation. They have worked a long time at this, to get the "shape" right. Now they move smoothly across the room to music. Their concentration is a wonderful thing to see. But suddenly, when the group reaches the other side, Michael calls out, "Hey, we can't *turn around* to go back. Ferry boats don't turn around. We'll have to walk backwards!" Somehow, none of the children had realized this before. Another child then perceives another problem. "Well, what happens to the man who steers the ferry up there in the little house on top? Doesn't he turn around?"

HAROLD: There are *two* little houses. The man walks to the other end when it is time to go back across the river.

MICHAEL: I don't remember seeing *two* little houses.

TEACHER: Well, that's another thing for us to find out when we go to the river tomorrow. We'll take a good look at a ferry, and that will settle the question.

Here, in this ideal classroom, Michael does not have to keep entirely still or sit still very much of the time. His natural impulse to move, and his impulses to act, to play, to pretend, are used and built upon.

47

And What About Reading?

Of course, there is reading in the curriculum—when the children are ready for it. But reading is by no means the major activity. It is, let us say, a part of the major activity, integrated with it and taking its meaning from it. Children who are busy exploring their neighborhood will have a real eagerness to be able to read the writing on the mail truck, the name on the ferry boat, the warning posted on the drawbridge. They will want to be able to write a letter to the postman, inviting him to come and talk to their class. They will want to be able to read the letter he sends them.

But never does the process of sitting and reading out of a book become the goal, the be-all and end-all of the curriculum, even for those children who are very eager to read. On the other hand, the keynote can best be expressed in a few words and phrases that carry a flavor of the *attitude* we are trying to foster in our children— such words and phrases as "intellectual curiosity," "first-hand investigation," "eagerness to explore and track down answers," "digesting information by actively *using* it in creative ways, not just soaking it in passively," "critical thinking," "enthusiasm."

This is no classroom for a child who is *not* alert, independent, active, imaginative, dramatic. For Michael— and thank goodness, most young children are like him if given a chance—for Michael does it not lay the foundation for the kind of thinking and living that make for vitality in a democratic society?

¶ TWO CLASSROOMS
And Two Kinds of Discipline

Teachers sometimes say, "How can you have any discipline when you let children get noisy and walk all around the room, the way they're supposed to do in the schools these days? If you stop being firm with children, you're going to have bedlam, and I just don't believe in it."

It is a common misconception that the teacher in the new type of education must relinquish firmness and discipline when she lets children "walk all around the room." Of course bedlam will result if the adults in charge "stop being firm," and of course bedlam has no place in the schoolroom. Teachers are quite right in wanting to avoid a situation such as this:

SCENE I

A FIRST GRADE ROOM

These children have been studying the transportation and handling of milk, from its source in the country to its delivery to the school. They have been to watch the bottling process in the Borden plant in their neighborhood. Now they are attempting to construct out of boxes and cartons some trucks and trains, and a school building and a bottling plant, so that they can play out the whole process.

Sounds fine, doesn't it, but how does it work?

We open the door and look in, and indeed, complete bedlam is just about all we hear and see. It is the beginning of the "work period," and the teacher, Miss O., is trying to help the children get started at their various jobs. But every child seems to be talking at the top of his lungs, and most of the children are sitting at their seats waving their arms and legs around, working at nothing —except making little paper airplanes, or poking each other. Miss O. is reading off the names of the committees that have been assigned to construct the various parts of the project, but the children seem to pay little attention to her, in spite of the fact that she is practically shouting to make herself heard over their noise. In the midst of all this, Arthur leaps onto another boy and

begins a real fight down in the aisle. Miss O. stops trying to get the rest of the children to work, and begins to talk to Arthur:

"Arthur, *sit down!* Stop fighting!"

The boys ignore her. She claps her hands loudly, but still the boys do not heed her, and the noise grows throughout the class. Miss O. starts over toward the fighting boys, but on the way a little girl comes up and asks for help on cutting through a stiff piece of cardboard. Miss O. pauses a moment to help, and then is diverted by Jimmy who is making quite a mess at his desk with the paste. She stops to give him some directions about cleaning it up. Meanwhile Arthur goes on furiously pummeling, and other children are gathering around to see this fight. When Miss O. finally gets around to separating the boys, the fight has gone on for at least five minutes.

Not Enough To Do

Gradually the children drift to their work, one group of three or four attempting to construct a train, another the school building, and so on. Their lack of interest seems to stem from the fact that they do not have quite enough to do. One child in each "committee" gets hold of his carton, and there is nothing else for the rest of his group to work on. Arthur, for instance, seizes upon one of the three pairs of scissors that are available for the whole class, and begins cutting out the windows on the "bottling plant." He is a big strong boy, bigger than the other three in his committee. These boys stand around and ask for turns to cut, but he hangs on tightly to the scissors, and will let no one else have a chance. Finally these discouraged boys leave the group, walking aimlessly up and down, sailing paper airplanes around, and tussling with each other.

After a while Arthur gets tired of cutting and decides to sweep the floor. It has become so late today, though, that Miss O. wants to omit the sweeping up. She asks Arthur to put away the broom and get on his coat and hat. He has developed a habit of ignoring what she says, however, and pays no attention to her. Miss O. finally gives up the attempt to stop him and tries to get the children lined up by the door. But the few who are able to stay quietly in line for a few moments get discouraged waiting for the straggling noisy ones, and soon they, too, begin to hop and jump around. Finally Miss O. asks all the children to take their seats in order to quiet down. It takes a long time to get the whole class seated. The bell has already rung, but still the children are not ready. "Quiet! Quiet!" shouts Miss O., but in vain.

Here, indeed, is a room where, during this work period at any rate, there is literal bedlam. Here is a teacher who not only fails to organize the work adequately for the children, but is *not* firm with them. She shouts at them, to be sure, in an attempt to be firm. But in reality she is not firm, because she does not follow through and really see that the children do the things she asks them to. The children are quick to perceive this weakness, and cannot resist taking advantage of her, much as they like her. They are accomplishing very little and Arthur, for one, is becoming a regular young bully. Surely no one could possibly feel that this kind of atmosphere is a very healthy one for children—though indeed it is much to the teacher's credit that she is genuinely fond of the children and does not try to discipline them by threats or harsh punishment.

Must activity in the schoolroom mean an atmosphere such as this?

Not at all.

There can be activity, and firmness on the teacher's part at the same time. Indeed, there must be.

What is "firmness"?

There are, perhaps, a number of different kinds. One of the old-fashioned kinds aimed at frightening and scaring children. The firmness used by the skillful teacher in the new schoolroom, on the other hand, is apt to be such a pleasant firmness that the onlooker may scarcely realize it is there. But indeed it is there. This new teacher does not feel that the children need to be kept rigidly quiet and still, nor made to fear her and the principal—but neither does she let it become possible for them to run away with the necessary rules, or to find themselves at loose ends, or to create bedlam.

How does she do this?

Watch her—

SCENE II
ANOTHER FIRST GRADE ROOM

When we look into this room, where desks have been removed, the children are sitting grouped around the teacher, Miss P., for a story and a discussion preceding the work period. The story is an exciting one about the adventure of a milkman and his horse. The 25 children, though they are sitting in a close little group, are entirely still, all their attention on the story. Not one of them is sitting with folded hands. Their teacher does not require them to do so. And why should she? The hands of these absorbed children are bothering no one.

The story comes to an end, and the teacher begins to plan the next period with the children. Some of them are very eager to get to work, and have a natural restlessness after the quiet story period. Miss P. asks the children not to get up until all the plans are made, but some of them do get up anyway, and start carrying their chairs back to their tables. They appear not to have understood Miss P., or to have their minds so intent upon getting to work that they have no ears for anything else. For a moment, there is what might be called a slight amount of bedlam—some children jumping up with their chairs, and trying to walk past the other children who are sitting; a chair accidentally knocked over; other children trying to talk to Miss P.

But right here is the test of Miss P. Is she going to make Miss O.'s mistake of *not following through her directions?* Will she let the children go ahead and start work even though she has asked them to sit and make plans first? It would be easy just to let the children go fumbling ahead, since they have already started, but this way of getting to work is the disorganized, difficult way for the class. These young children are not yet capable of organizing their day, and they really need the teacher's help. Does Miss P. have skill enough to keep hold of the reins? In other words, does she have the essential firmness, or doesn't she?

Yes, she has it.

The Right Kind of Firmness

"Why children," she calls, loudly so that they can all hear, but not unpleasantly, "Marcia, Tyrone, Sylvia—we didn't say it was time yet to go to work. You didn't understand. We aren't through planning what work we're going to do. Bring your chairs back. That's right."

It takes time to call these children back, to insist that they return with their chairs and sit in them once again, but this is exactly what is required of the successful teacher—patience enough to really carry out the things she says. We might call this the first principle.

The children all do return and sit down. The group is quiet once more. (Children usually do cooperate willingly with a teacher who has this pleasant firmness.) Plans are completed rapidly, and the children then proceed to their work without any confusion. Miss P. has saved the day, not only by organizing it for the children but by insisting that they adhere to this organization. This does not mean, of course, that the children have no leeway to help organize, to help make plans, and to choose the kind of work they want to do. It does not mean that Miss P. is an autocrat. It *does* mean that she provides the firmness that all children really want and need in adults: she will not let them do the things that lead to confusion, license, bedlam. She is a prop, a help, a strength to them, without which they are not yet capable of managing themselves. And indeed, the peaceful atmosphere which she insists on in turn reacts upon her, and makes her a much more relaxed and calm person than Miss O. could possibly be in the midst of her bedlam.

"But," you ask, "is the day really saved? What happens during the work period? Don't the children get awfully noisy?"

Let's see.

The Right Kind of Activity

These children have been studying their neighborhood in relation to their school. The center of activity seems to be a playhouse in one corner of the room. Several children are now busy constructing furniture for this house. Each one of these children has an orange crate to work on, with hammer and nails. Others are painting orange crate furniture. One boy pretends to deliver a truck full of coal to the house. Several are down on the floor playing with blocks. Their play, too, seems to center around coal and its delivery.

Every child in the room is busy at something—such as blocks, clay, painting, carpentry, or dramatic play in the playhouse.

Wait a moment—did we say every child? Here is one boy, Henry, who seems to be dashing around the room. He goes from one group of children to another, poking around to see what others are doing. He seems to be a bit "wild"—look at him rolling aimlessly on the floor.

"Ah," you say. "This is exactly what's apt to happen. The children get wild and some of them just have to be held down. There are bound to be children like Arthur and Henry in every class."

Well, let's see what Henry's teacher thinks about it. Here she comes. Is she going to scold him? Discipline him? Hold him down?

"Why, Henry, did we forget to plan for you? Let's see, what was your job? I believe we both forgot. Oh, I know—you were going to paint the sofa, weren't you? There are a lot of extra paint brushes up on my desk."

Henry gets right up, finds his paint brush, and starts to work at once with zest, all wildness forgotten. All he needed was a little help in getting started on a job that interested him.

Perhaps this could be formulated as the second important principle: Children need to have work to do that interests them—*enough* to do, *a lot* to do. Interested, busy, happy children are almost always self-controlled children, with neither time nor inclination for wildness. In Miss O.'s room the activity was not organized in such a way as to give *each child* work to do. There were not enough scissors to go around, and some of the children had to just stand and watch for the whole period while others of their committees worked on the construction of the buildings. This is expecting too much of young children. Miss P. has realized this and has given each child some piece of work to do.

But let's go back to the point about noise. Do these children get too noisy? Yes, sometimes they do, of course, what with hammers banging, voices talking freely, blocks clattering on the floor. This does not mean, though, that the teacher needs to let the volume of noise rise to a point at which it creates real tension in the atmosphere. There are ways of controlling it.

Bedlam Isn't Necessary

Miss P. goes to her piano when she feels the noise is too much. She has one particular little phrase she plays as a "signal." The children hear it and stop work and look up. "Who remembers what this means?" Miss P. asks.

"We're getting too noisy," pipes up Ronnie.

The children seem to like this musical "signal," and they accept it as a reasonable one. Indeed, they helped to work it out with the teacher in the first place, agreeing that they needed some kind of reminder, and choos-

ing the phrase they wanted her to play for the signal. Now they really are much quieter as they resume their work. Of course, there continues to be what might be called "normal noise" in the room—the noise of children feeling free to talk with each other, work and play together in a spontaneous way. It is necessary to distinguish between this healthy noise and the unhealthy noise of bedlam. There is no doubt about it, a teacher must expect a certain amount of "noise" if she is to have constructive activity in her room. Eliminate all noise, and you also must eliminate many of the learnings, both social and intellectual, that grow out of situations in which children are free to talk and play naturally.

"Normal Noise" Is Good

For instance, look at these three children down on the floor playing with the blocks. Tyrone is running a train on a track, Ronnie has his little truck filled with "coal," and is delivering it to Josephine's "house." They accompany their play with a constant stream of talk, but who would say that this is idle chatter? This is, in fact, *thinking* and *learning* and *planning together*:

"That's a track and a truck can't go on a track, can it?" "How could a truck go through a house? You'll have to make the street go around. . . . But really you should push the house back so the street can be straight."

"Is this where the coal man comes? Looks like the bedroom to me. Your bed is too close to the furnace. It will catch on fire!"

Who would sacrifice good thinking such as this for the sake of a completely quiet room?

"But don't you have to insist on complete quietness to get children through some of the routines of getting their wraps on, or of cleaning things up when they are through?"

57

How does Miss P. manage the clean-up period and dismissal?

She is walking over to the piano now. The work period is over. She plays a chord on the piano to get the children's attention, and does not speak until all the children do look up at her.

"Children, I'm sorry now we have to stop and clean up, but I want to tell you how proud I am of all of you. You've all been working so beautifully, we've had one of our very best work periods. And now I know you can clean up just as well."

How we thrive on praise, all of us! Children do hate to stop work and play in which they are interested, but praise and encouragement like this are equivalent to getting the clean-up job half done. The children scurry around efficiently and willingly, without much noise or confusion, and are soon ready to get their coats on and line up by the door.

This dismissal procedure goes quickly too, though Miss P. has at no time asked the children to be com-

Today it is snowing

pletely quiet. In fact, she has done just the opposite. She stands near the door with those who have already lined up, and talks with them and plays a little game with them, to keep them from the natural restlessness and noise that they might drift into if required just to stand and wait idly for the slower children. (Remember, that is what happened in Miss O.'s room!)

"Children, do you remember our shoemaker game?" Miss P. says. "Henry, you show us the sound the shoemaker's hammer makes." Henry makes his little tapping sound (a wonderful imitation!). "Ronnie, you show us the polishing sound. . . . Sylvia, do you remember the sound the machine made? Now let's all make the sounds together. We can imagine then that the shoemaker's shop is right here in this room!"

The children, of course, take great delight in this sound game, which is not a very noisy game even though it does involve making sounds, and they have no difficulty standing in line waiting for the slower children.

Waiting, for them, is not an idle restless time. Miss P. has made it even an interesting time. The slow children hurry with their wraps so they can play the game too. In just a moment all of the children are ready to walk out into the hall, without the slightest bit of confusion. Another important principle is at work here: Miss P. knows that she will be struggling against a very strong current if she expects these young children to stand or sit quietly for more than just a few moments with nothing to occupy their hands or minds. Of course, if she wanted to frighten the children into being quiet, she could do so.

In summary, what are the principles a teacher such as Miss P. holds to, to prevent bedlam yet give her children opportunity for active work and play?

Firmness on the teacher's part is as necessary to young children in the new type of classroom as it ever was in

59

the old. But it does not imply crossness or harshness or autocratic discipline. It means that the children can depend on the teacher to help them organize, help them control themselves, help them avoid bedlam and license.

Self-controlled children are busy, interested children, who have a lot of absorbing, active work of their own to do.

"Signals," games, encouragement and praise make for a happy, friendly atmosphere in which children willingly cooperate with the teacher. They sense that she is co-operating with them—that she is sympathetic to their needs and "on their side."

Children are apt to cooperate readily in carrying out the rules and regulations if they themselves have had some part in deciding what these rules shall be. Not all rules, of course, can be handed over to small children to make. But many opportunities can be found for the children's participating (such as deciding on a "quiet signal").

A teacher must work along *with* and not *against* the strong physical need of young children to keep moving.

SECOND GRADE
SCENES

¶ THOSE BOYS, And Their War Pictures

It is a free period. In this particular second grade room at the present time the children are left pretty much to their own devices during this period. They are free to crayon pictures, to work in their work books, to paste and cut, and to carry out little construction projects of their own.

Today a good many of the children—boys especially— are crayoning pictures. They sit there at their desks contented, relaxed, working at their drawings with care and concentration and obvious enjoyment. Their teacher has wisely left them to draw in their own way without instruction or models to copy.

Let's look over the shoulders of these children and see what kind of pictures they are making with such intent interest.

Here is George's—American planes dropping bombs on an enemy ship.

Henry's—a fierce battle scene, with guns shooting, planes crashing.

Caruso's—another picture of planes and warships, all very carefully executed, with dotted lines criss-crossing intricately to show the exact paths of the bombs and torpedoes.

Yes, war, war and war again, not only today but almost any day and every day when these children are free to draw pictures.

Their teacher explains: "The boys never seem to get tired of these war pictures. I figure that it's a pretty real interest, so I just let them go ahead and draw them."

She is undoubtedly right in feeling that war is a real interest to these children. Many of them have relatives who have seen war service, and they are children who go frequently to movies of any and every kind. On all sides of them war has impinged upon them, exciting them and troubling them.

There could hardly be any doubt that they really need some opportunity to play war, to talk about war, and to draw war pictures. In doing so, they are working off some of their excitement, bringing out into the open some of their concern. The suppression of this emotionally charged interest would only serve to create one of many types of problems in the children.

And, too, as they draw war pictures they are probably satisfying other strong urges that have nothing to do with war.

They're After Something More

What were 7-year-old boys playing and drawing in the days before World War II?

Not daisies and buttercups, of that we can be sure. Those were the days of cowboys and G-Men and desperadoes and supermen. (Of course, Superman is still very much alive, war or no war.) Can you not recall seeing groups of young children out on the street playing dramatic games that smacked very much of the radio dramas and the comics—games involving buried treasures and hide-outs and narrow escapes and heroic rides? Cops, robbers, drownings, and dangers of all kinds?

Our 7-year-old children today draw endless war pictures *partly* because they are after what they have always been after—excitement, adventure, a feeling of mastery over the most dangerous things they can think of, a sense of power. (The reasons why they are after these things may be rather complex and we do not need to go into them at present.)

The question occurs at once: Are we really doing our educational best by the children by allowing them to satisfy these strong urges solely by drawing war pictures day in and day out? Do we take these urges into consideration when we plan our curriculum? If our children have a strong need to identify themselves with daredevil, powerful heroes, is it not up to us to recognize this need and meet it in as many constructive ways as possible, within the very framework of the curriculum?

Let no one think that the neighborhood streets hold no possibilities for drama and excitement and the challenge of danger! If we have failed to make our second grade neighborhood studies as interesting to the children as the concern with bombings and shootings, possibly it is partly because we have been too utilitarian, too sober, too matter of fact. Perhaps we ourselves have been blind to the exciting vistas.

Right on Our Own Streets

Have we helped our children to see the neighborhood firemen as the "supermen" many of them really are? Do we lead the children to inquire into the nature of the fireman's training? Is there a 7-year-old who would not thrill to the picture of a fireman learning to balance himself on narrow window ledges, learning to shoot guns that send ropes up to people trapped on roofs, learning to jump into nets, climb swinging ladders, drive with speed through crowded streets?

And what about our study of the trains that bring food to our city? Do we keep this purely on the informational level, considering only the functions of the trains? Do we ever consider the life of the railroad engineer, the hazards of the job, the possible dangers of wrecks, floods, breakdowns? Do we lead the children to investigate the wonderful workings of train signals? These things can be as exciting to 7-year-olds as any war.

And what about our river traffic? Boats are fascinating at any age, and the 7-year-old's interest in them is surely not confined to those that are equipped with guns. The Hudson, at our very doors, has its currents, its channels, its lighthouse, its ice in the winter, its dangers and signals that every pilot must learn.

And take the mundane matter of the subway. Seven-year-olds are not too young to sense the gigantic achievement involved in the construction of a subway that leaves undisturbed all the complicated underground world of water mains, sewer pipes, gas pipes, power lines. Many of these children have an avid interest in the fantastic "underground" world inhabited by characters in the comics. How about showing them a little of the real and no less fascinating "underground" world here under their own sidewalks?

Marvels, Here and Now

And what about the other miracles in our everyday things? When we study milk with our children, do we teach them merely to be able to recite that milk comes

64

from cows in the country, and is carried to the city on trains? Let's take the class, if possible, to see one of these bottling and capping machines. Watch the children's eyes pop with wonder at the mechanized march of the bottles—over a hundred filled with milk in one minute, then mechanically capped, mechanically placed in delivery cases! Surely our 7's, who like to plot out the paths of bombs and torpedoes, cannot fail to respond with keen interest to the efficiency, the speed, the intricacy of this wonderful bottling machine.

And let's not forget the marvels of the physical as well as of the industrial world.

Remember, these children, as they draw, are in their imaginations heroically killing hundreds of spies, tricking the enemy, rising successfully out of hazardous bombing dives. Let's give them a little chance to manipulate nature—let them learn how to balance a toy boat by putting on a keel; let them discover how to make water run up hill; give them a few simple experiments in which they can learn how to harness powerful steam.

We are not saying, of course, that the children should not be allowed to go on drawing their war pictures. We repeat, the war has been an important part of their world, and the drawing of these pictures is not only a harmless but also a healthy means of expression, serving a number of useful functions. The war pictures have a legitimate place in our schools, but they should not be the only source of satisfaction of the children's need for dangerous challenge and achievement. We are unnecessarily limiting our children's world, if we leave matters this way.

Perhaps we cannot compete so successfully with the war world and the world of the comics that we can entirely erase the need for Superman or the spy killer and persuade the children to substitute the fireman in his place. There is no need to. What we can do, and should do, is give the children a taste of a curriculum that has the breath of life in it. Let's take a cue from the children and include a generous infusion of the elements of excitement and daring and heroic challenge in our studies of the everyday world.

¶ LUCILE, Who Doesn't Do Her Work

She's an attractive, lively little seven-year-old girl, neatly and nicely dressed. Her bright expression leads us to believe at once that her trouble, whatever it may be, is *not* stupidity.

Let's take a look into her notebook. What neat figures, what neatly written rows of spelling words! Of course, the pages are scantily filled, we see, when we compare her notebook with those of the other children. But no one could complain that she does not know how to do her work. The trouble seems to be that she *will* not.

"Day after day it is the same," her teacher says. "She will not stay in her seat and do her work, but is constantly up bothering the other children, teasing them and trying to get them to play with her. . . . Her mother says she never has got along well with other children, and acts pretty spoiled at home. She doesn't mind there any better than she does here. I simply am not able to make her sit at her desk and pay attention to her work. What am I to do?"

What Is She Up To?

We can see for ourselves that Lucile is not doing her school work. It is an arithmetic period now. For a few moments Lucile writes examples in her notebook as the others do, then she is up grabbing a pencil away from Dorothy, in front of her. . . . Back to her seat for a moment, but only a moment, and then she leaves the room with the teacher's permission. When she returns, several children are at the blackboard writing sums. Lucile strolls curiously up to Margaret and watches her write "123." When Margaret turns her back Lucile picks up the eraser and rubs out the sum. Of course that makes Margaret angry, and the two of them begin to scrap with each other. The teacher tells them both to sit down, but Lucile manages not to go directly to her seat. She picks up a piece of chalk and writes on top of Rita's figures, scrawling lightly over the "145." In the next moment she and Rita are chasing each other around the room, more or less playfully.

The arithmetic period is nearly over, and as usual Lucile has accomplished nothing—nothing academic, that is. She has managed, however, to make several contacts for herself with other children.

Yes, obviously she is much more interested in her relationships with the other children than she is in her school work at present. But is this a situation that can be toler-

ated in the schoolroom? Just what practical steps can the teacher take? What *should* she do? Surely she cannot allow Lucile to snatch pencils all day long. Surely the child should be helped to cover at least a minimum of the academic ground?

Of course. Yet it is clear to see that the social relationships have a real urgency for Lucile at the present time, and should not be ignored.

Emotions Have a Place

It is all too easy for us to think of the children in our classes as receptive little minds, ready to learn arithmetic, writing, and reading. We forget that these children come to us as *people*. They do not take their emotions off with their coats and hang them in the cloak closet. They bring their physical, emotional, and social needs right into the classroom, and these are often much more compelling to them than their academic needs.

It may be that Lucile has not found a very satisfactory way to play with other children—she seems always to tease—and that she is very much concerned with this problem of working out a better relationship. We know that seven is an age when children begin to form a feeling of themselves as a group, apart from and even lined up against the adult world. (This may partly explain Lucile's resistance both at school and at home.) They are not content to establish individual relationships between themselves and the teacher. They must establish places for themselves within the group of children, and this is an imperative matter to them.

Lucile's teacher might well look around at her classroom and ask herself whether she is allowing the children any opportunity for free social interchange, for the chance to get acquainted, to measure themselves up in a personal way, one against another, or to find out where they stand in the eyes of their fellows and for what reasons.

Lucile, for all we know, may be trying to find out if she can get along with her classmates in the teasing, dominating way that she does at home.

Or she may be eager for friendships that she does not know how to begin in any other way.

And, too, there may be other much deeper reasons underlying this teasing, social urge, reasons which cannot be probed in a day.

This should not discourage the teacher, however. There are some practical steps she can take at once, whether or not she understands all of the reasons underlying Lucile's behavior. It is at least clear that Lucile needs *more*, not *less*, opportunity to try her wings in this area of social relationships.

First Steps

A good beginning might be made by including in the daily program a time when the children may be free to talk together for a while about the things that interest them, even if it's no more than the new teeth they're getting. What about the milk period? May the children sit in groups and talk at that time? And what about recess? Is this an entirely regimented period, when all the groups must play formal singing games together? Can something be done about that?

Lucile's teacher might even make progress in two ways if she could let Lucile work at her arithmetic with some other child for short periods; and if she could make up arithmetic games involving not only Lucile but other children.

Of course, Lucile may not settle down to her academic work immediately, even if she is given more legitimate opportunity to talk and play with the other children. The few suggestions listed here certainly may not constitute the complete tool for probing into and handling all of Lucile's problem.

But this is the way a teacher makes a beginning, picking her way step by step, following the leads that are the most obvious and the most practical; seeking the help of social worker or psychologist if necessary; adjusting her method of attack as she learns more about the child; and always remembering that school is a *social* place as well as an academic place, and that the social lessons are often difficult to learn, and have a legitimate place in the classroom.

By DOROTHY STALL:

Prologue

*Third and Fourth
Grade Children*

By the time a child is eight or nine his world is expanding in many ways. He finds his own way to school, chooses his own friends, helps to care for the younger ones at home. He is likely to quote the teacher to his parents, assert his own ideas with great assurance, and be quite free with criticisms of adults.

He has traveled a little perhaps, and knows where trains and boats and airplanes go. He has developed a lively imagination based on his eight or nine years of varied experience.

A child born in a big city enters the complicated civilization of a mechanized world. For the first few years it takes all his energy and thought, just finding out how everything works, where things go, what they are for, how to manipulate them. There is no concept of any other kind of civilization, any other way of life, even of any other place except that in which he lives.

But gradually he hears of other places, and vague pictures begin to form in his mind. Perhaps a friend of

the family comes from far away. He hears stories of other lands, looks at pictures. He sees people who reflect other places and other ways. He begins to study differences, to search for reasons.

And then he begins to wonder about himself and ask about his beginnings, who his parents were, and their parents. And he asks many things about himself of himself, and often no one knows what he is asking. Sometimes he asks in very roundabout ways. What nationality would he be if his father were French, his mother American, and if he had been born on an ocean liner half-way between the two countries?

And then he begins to ask about the whole world. How it got started. Who was the father of the very first person, and if God made the very first person, then who made God? And it pleases him to discover in reading the very old tales from all over the world that people everywhere wanted to know these same things. He feels kinship with them and yet apart, more advanced, because there is science in his world.

Both stories and experience stimulate his imagination further. The hill he has climbed can easily become a snow-capped mountain, the trickling brook in the park a raging torrent.

His feelings too can expand with imaginative power. In sawing through a tough board he is Superman. Pitching a beautiful game brings him all the glory of an idealized sports hero. Acting in a play gives an opportunity to express complex emotions without embarrassment.

There is no limit to the dreams of growing up, of proving one's strength, of being loved, of gaining recognition. And they are not just dreams.

Children of eight and nine can take real responsibility, solve many problems without feeling overburdened. They can to a great extent help create their own school world, a world which they enjoy. They begin to learn to rule themselves as a group, to find a place in which their abilities count. Dreams and growth go hand in hand.

As they study about those who have struggled with nature, overcome hardship, and conquered superstition, they also discover their own powers of courage and insight. They are eager to learn more and more about this amazing and complicated world, and even beyond it, into the mysteries of the larger universe.

As they grow older they also become more aware of the feelings of others. There are times when they may choose their own partners, other times when they must take responsibility for a weaker or younger child; times when they may make their own choices, others when the teacher must plan for them; times when they may use all the materials they want, others when a hammer and saw must be shared.

In the following pages some of these eight- and nine-year-old children come to life, with clashing, with contrast, with beauty, and with that diversity which makes the study of personality such a rewarding adventure.

We find here children who are strong and able to be themselves, others who have had to build up a false front.

There are those compelled to grab and hoard, others who are relaxed and happy sharing materials.

There are some who must win approval through blind conforming, others who are able to help build their own norms.

There are children unable to create anything original, who feel safe only when they imitate, but others who are free and spontaneous in creative language and art.

There are some who must wield power over others in order to feel strong, but many who can live and let live, because they are secure.

We find a few who must pile up a mountain of isolated facts, and yet a majority who appreciate learning how to think, and who are able to enjoy the rich life and culture of their own and their story-book world.

If conditions are healthy and guidance is wise, eight- and nine-year-old children will listen to each other and to the teacher as well. They will grow and flower as individuals, each according to the laws of his own personality. They will also learn to enjoy group thinking, group work and organized play.

THIRD GRADE SCENES

THIRD GRADE
SCENES

¶ GEORGIE, Who Wanted The Teacher
To Be Like A Mother

Every class and every age has a Georgie. But a Georgie
in the beginning of Third Grade, a Georgie who is still
seven, and in his emotional development even more like
six, can be very appealing, in spite of the difficulties he
creates.

This Georgie is like that, and now he is listening to a
story. So are all the others, sitting relaxed even in the
screwed-down seats. The teacher is sitting too, in an
ordinary chair up front. Now she gets up to show a
picture, continuing to read as she walks up and down
the aisle.

This satisfies everyone but Georgie. Georgie follows
at her heels, and when she sits down again, Georgie is
there leaning over her shoulder, to be first to see the next
picture, and just to feel near.

Comfortably he leans his arm over her chair, and
occasionally tries to engage her in private conversation.

"Oh, sit down," cries a child in an irritated voice. "*We*
want to hear the story."

"Back to your seat now, Georgie," the teacher reminds
him kindly. And he goes. But he doesn't stay. Soon he
is running up again, and she must stop to speak to him.

But he doesn't want to leave her, until the sharp voices of the children call him back again.

Going for a Walk

How does Georgie get along in other situations? We watch him now as the class lines up for a walk to the river. The children are choosing partners, running to grab each other's hands. But no one chooses Georgie.

It doesn't seem to bother him. He looks a little bewildered. But he keeps looking at the teacher as if waiting for her to tell him what to do.

"You be Georgie's partner, Ruth," the teacher suggests. Ruth groans and screws up her face.

"But Mollie's going to be my partner," she protests, reaching out her hand as Mollie comes sliding down the aisle toward her.

Georgie looks crestfallen.

"All right," the teacher says cheerfully, "you'll be my partner." And Georgie happily goes with the teacher to the front of the line.

"He's always first!" the two in front complain. The teacher ignores their remarks and they start out.

But when they get out on the street, Georgie holds

them back. He wants to look in the window longer than anyone else, and must be urged along. He sometimes wanders off and becomes absorbed in some small stick floating down the gutter, and they all have to wait until the teacher brings him back. They are all eager to get down to the river.

Georgie or Group?

The teacher has a real problem here. There is a conflict between Georgie's needs and the needs of the group. After all, why shouldn't the children resent being held back? Why shouldn't they be jealous of Georgie's close relationship with the teacher? For many of them, this sort of thing happens at home with a younger brother or sister, and they have to pretend to be very grown up, and not to care. But this is school, a class where all are equal.

Georgie's feelings must be hurt when the other children are so annoyed with him, when they refuse to be his partner, when they yell at him along the street.

The teacher understands this. She wants to meet Georgie's need to be mothered as best she can. But she also has obligations to the group.

What Are Some Of The Things A Teacher Can Do?

The teacher knows that Georgie needs to be near her. And yet she also knows that he needs to grow up. The other children need to feel that she is fair to them all, and yet they need to learn to be kind to a weaker child.

Perhaps if she seats him in the front row near her desk that will help. He will be near enough to feel companionship, and to speak to her privately, without exposing his immaturities to the rest of the class. Perhaps his mother will tell her something that will make her understand Georgie a little better.

It's Easy To Understand!

The opportunity comes one rainy day. Georgie's mother comes rushing in at the noon hour, while the children are having lunch in the big room. The teacher is not on lunch duty so she has a moment to talk.

"Here are his rain-coat and rubbers," the mother says breathlessly. "I ran home to get them during my lunch hour. Lucky I work nearby. It didn't look a bit like rain this morning."

The teacher invites the mother to rest a bit before she returns to her job.

"It's hard," the mother says as she sits back in the chair, "to be a father and mother both to a growing child."

The teacher does not probe, but the story soon comes. Georgie's father was killed in the war. The teacher listens with deep sympathy.

Then, looking nervously at her watch, the mother rises to go.

"Thank you for being so kind," she says. "I can see he is in good hands. Do see that no one teases him, won't you? I'm afraid he can't stick up very well for himself."

Here the children come now, back from lunch. Georgie's mother pulls him aside and clings to him. Then, reluctantly, she lets him go. She will be late to work.

The Class Is There, Too!

The teacher's thoughts are full of Georgie and his mother. But she has to stop thinking about him now. For there is her class and she must plan for each child.

She must find out who can read well and with understanding; which children need exercises for comprehension; who still sees words reversed and mixes up *was* and *saw;* and if there are any who have only just barely caught on to reading.

What does Georgie do while she is struggling with all these things? He is just watching, and waiting for her exclusive attention. But she must observe the others now, so she asks him to draw until she can come to him.

Little Time To Think In School

It is not until she is on her way home that Georgie can find a place in her thoughts again. And walking through the park she wonders. She must gradually wean him away from so much dependence on her. She must help him learn to use his own initiative. She must help him work along with the other children and make friends with the other children, so he will feel he really belongs.

There is a table with four small chairs in a corner where the children can "play house." There are orange crates standing on end for cupboards. There are toy dishes, an iron, some folded bright cloths, and other house-play objects. Not much for a boy.

At home the teacher searches through her scraps for things Georgie might find interesting in connection with a house. She digs out an old length of brass tubing, a length of rubber hose, a coil of wire, some old tire tape. And when she goes out to shop for supper, she stops at the ten-cent store for a small pulley and some clothes-line rope. With these things to add to the scrap-box in school, perhaps Georgie can find a role to play as "man around the house."

A Set-Up For Georgie

A few children are working at their desks with plasticene. Others at the blackboard are drawing with colored chalk. Some are working with crayons at their desks, and three children are painting scenery for a skit about what they did during the summer vacation. The teacher has carefully chosen a group to play house with Mary. Georgie is one of them.

"Georgie," the teacher calls, "here are some things to add to our scrap-box. If anything in the house needs fixing, now you've got things to do it with."

Georgie is delighted and comes running for the things. But Bill is delighted too. He runs and grabs the length of hose and the pulley and rope before Georgie has a chance to think twice. However, they both run to Mary to show her these new possessions. The teacher is watching now to see what happens.

Bill has put the scrap-box on a desk near Mary, and now he is fishing through it for more gadgets.

"Want an electric socket for your iron?" Bill calls to Mary, who has turned back to her sewing after glancing at the new things. She is making a pair of curtains for the cupboard.

While Bill and two other boys start fitting things together, Georgie pulls up a chair near Mary. "I'll watch you," he says contentedly.

Is he just pretending to be content, the teacher wonders, because he isn't tough enough to cope with these boys?

But now they are away from the box and Georgie gets up. He fishes around too, for something to "fix." Up he comes with an old spigot. "Hey, Mary, here's a water faucet for your wash tub!"

Mary beams. Georgie sits near her again and begins to fit the rubber hose onto the spigot. "What you doing?" one of the boys turns to ask.

"Water faucet," Georgie exclaims. "See?"

Now he is sticking the end of the hose through a crack in the orange crate.

"Look, look," Bill calls out, and the others crowd around.

"You need a water tank to put on top," one suggests.

"Wait, I'll get that old can," another cries, running to the big corner cupboard. Soon he is back with it.

"Here you are, Georgie. Let me help?"

Well, here is the beginning, the teacher feels. And she watches while they beg for turns to help Georgie. One holds the can while Georgie punches a hole for the hose with a hammer and screw driver. They all give ideas and work it out together. This really is a beginning.

There Are Other Ways, Too

It is not only in dramatic play that Georgie can be helped to grow up. There are special errands involving responsibility, such as being asked to take the small clock to the office and set it; playing the leading part in Giant Steps; leading the class on an adventure through part of the park; helping another child in writing, at which he happens to be very good; beating the drum with a special rhythm of his own, while the class marches or dances to it; learning to choose his own activity from a list; getting out his own materials and working without so much help; following directions when his group works together.

If Georgie's mother knows he is happy in school, it will ease her burden somewhat. And the warm relationship between the teacher, his mother, and his classmates can make Georgie feel he lives in a friendly world.

¶ A CLASS, Cramped and Divided

This teacher said, "I don't see how I can ever take this class on a trip! There are so many children with problems. They pick at each other all the time. And the cliques! Why, if one group thinks the other has two minutes longer for a game they are ready to pull hair over it. How can I take a class like that on the subway? I'd have a fight on my hands right in the middle of the aisle."

They Were Terribly Cramped

This teacher's problem was real. She was responsible for the children's safety. She *would* be taking a risk to take a trip too soon.

Yet she knew that just such a happy experience could help weld the class together. She remembered the common thrill of adventure another class had experienced when she had taken them on the lower deck of a ferry and across the river when it was clogged with ice. They had anticipated the ferry's attack on each approaching ice cake and felt at one with the ferry and with each

83

other as they heard the crunching and the grinding under their feet.

But not with this class. Social attitudes would have to come first. She must think of other unifying experiences which were possible. But what? The class was so irritable. Not only did the children come from homes which were cramped and where living was frugal, but they could scarcely even call their classroom their own.

It was one of a set of classrooms with sliding doors which are sometimes all rolled back to form a big Assembly room.

"We just never know when our walls are going to disappear!" the teacher explained. "We can't count on privacy, and the children can't be enthusiastic about decorating the room when their work is so likely to be torn or destroyed.

"Not only that! There is the noise! Other classes need the little stage to practice their plays—and voices carry. Sometimes we have to leave our room and travel to the room of the class which is using the stage. It's hard enough with easygoing children ,but with these—it's just too discouraging."

Still, She Was Not One To Give Up!

"Something should certainly be done to give our children decent rooms and plenty of space," the teacher admitted. "Maybe I could have some of these desks taken out in spite of the Assembly. That would help a little. In the meantime, I'll have to do the best I can."

In the few quiet moments available, she read them the story of *Little Fox* since their social studies were to be based on the Manhattan Indians. The story told of Indian feasts, and how the Indians prepared their food. This gave the teacher an idea.

She asked the children if they would like to cook and eat some Indian food in the classroom. She knew this would be possible, and food was a good cure for many problems. After talking about succotash, parched corn, and oyster stew, the children decided to try parching corn. Of course, it would have to be done in a modern frying pan, and over an electric grill, but this was better than nothing. And the teacher suggested that they write a letter to a farmer in New Jersey to see if they could get some of last year's hard corn.

It took a week or two, and a trip by the teacher to the market, but they got the corn. A child brought the frying pan, and the teacher brought the grill. The children were full of anticipation. For once the attention of every child was focused on one activity.

"Now how shall we do it," the teacher asked, "so every one will have a turn?" At once there was a scurrying around, each child from the back trying to sit with someone up front. They all wanted to see at once. They all wanted the first turn. And why not?

"Oh!" thought the teacher, "if I could only get them into a circle. If I could only shove these desks around!"

"I'll call you three at a time to use the grill," she

promised. It looked and sounded like anarchy for a few minutes, as legs untwisted, shins bumped against iron supports of folding seats, and the children reshuffled themselves into groups of three. Out of the scramble the teacher quickly chose three, and helped them shell their corn right into the pan.

As the good popcorn smell began to fill the room, voices calmed down to a gentle hum of yum-yum sounds and delight. Still they all wanted to see. Some pushed forward, crowding each other in the aisle. The teacher had to watch that the children did not push near the hot grill.

One girl was shoved forcibly back by those who were next in line.

"Oh, who wants to eat that old burned corn anyway," she spluttered, and with a flip of her braids, stomped back to her own desk and pulled out a book. Others, becoming impatient, poked, pushed, and scowled and kept up a barrage of complaints.

"Why did I ever try this?" the teacher moaned to herself. "They can't wait for anything!" It took all the self-control she could muster not to yell "Sit down!"

But the first group finished and went to the back of the room to munch on this new delicacy, and they were quickly followed by those who had to wait their turns. This relieved the congestion at the front of the room. And soon she heard exclamations from the rear.

"Gee, the Indians knew a good thing when they had it!"

"Aw, let me taste just one! I'll give you one of mine when they're cooked!"

Before it was over, some were eating the grains raw, others digging them apart for scientific reasons. Others turned to drawing, or looked at picture books. But the homey smell of cooking kept them in fairly good spirits. It had been a success after all.

86

Other Unifying Experiences

The teacher made other brave attempts. There were more cooking experiments, including succotash and corn soup.

And after learning about the Indian's totem, the turtle, and the belief that a great turtle held up the earth, she took the class to a pet shop near the school. This was a way of taking a simple, easily controlled trip with this class of children.

They bought a turtle for a class pet, and organized themselves into the Clan of the Crawler, and Turtle Clan.

Each of these experiences seemed to help the children feel as one group, and they even began to hold council meetings to settle arguments when real trouble was brewing. They learned how to care for their pet, and sent a representative to each of the other classes in the "sliding-door" set-up to explain the significance of their pet, and to urge everyone to see that no harm came to it.

But an evil day came when the turtle disappeared. In spite of many meetings, searches, and investigations, it was never heard of again, and the effect on the class was most disheartening. They doubted that they could keep anything that was really their own.

After this the teacher began to think of new experiences to give the children something to enjoy together.

They all loved the George Washington Bridge which was near, and fortunately the site of the Bridge also held a world of meaning in terms of the Indians the children were studying.

The teacher began to talk about the possibilities of a big trip they might take in the spring to see Fort Washington Point under the George Washington Bridge where, according to Reginald Bolton,* "A considerable deposit of blackened soil, shells, and occasional scraps of

---

Indian Paths of the Great Metropolis by Reginald Bolton, p. 79.

87

pottery, gave evidence of an Indian fishing station and canoe landing place," in the long ago.

The children were very much excited about this, and began to concentrate their feelings and plans on the prospect of this trip. They also felt that since Alanson Skinner had found arrow points there, "probably lost in shooting the darting fish which swarmed the swirling tide around the famous headland," they too would find an arrow point when they searched the place.

They were led to imagine their neighborhood as it was in Indian times, and heard stories of now and long ago. When they talked about the building of the bridge, they read *The Little Red Lighthouse and the Great Gray Bridge*, by Hildegarde Hoyt Swift.

The children made table scenes, one with the neighborhood as it is today, one as they imagined it in Indian times. They made Indian figures from pipe cleaners and paper, and even dramatized Indian life with these as hand puppets. All of these activities, although in a small cramped way, helped to weld the class together.

And together they watched the weather reports in order to plan for the promised trip.

"Our Trip"

The day came and they all sat relaxed with anticipation holding their little brown paper lunch packages on their desks. The teacher called them, and they lined up. No pushing. No shoving. They were satisfied just to be going, going for a picnic at the old Indian site under the George Washington Bridge.

Their minds were full of images, their hopes high. They walked with a gay light step down the hall, and on behind their teacher to the subway. They kept in line so well, with a parent at the end to help, that the teacher scarcely felt the need to glance back often.

They had taken many short walks around the neigh-

borhood, and this was like a "graduation trip." It was the first they had taken together on the subway.

Once inside the subway car, Indian thoughts were temporarily forgotten. Every movement, every sound, made the children alert to the scene around them. They talked excitedly, showing off their knowledge to each other about what made the doors open and close, how fast the express was going as it passed the local, and all about the flashing, changing lights.

When the final station came, they made their way out with scarcely suppressed excitement. For high above their heads was a great arching roof, held up by mighty supports. There was an odor of being deep, deep down in the earth. They knew they were under the great hill of Washington Heights.

In line they followed their teacher onto the steep, crawling escalator. They were a little frightened, but enjoying their fright.

They stretched their necks and looked down at their long, long line, single file now in Indian style. They shivered at the thought of how deep, deep down beneath the hill they had really been. And there were shrieks of relief and delight as they reached the top and walked out into the light of day.

Around a windy corner they walked, and there was the great sweeping bridge in full view!

"The bridge! The bridge!" they cried. It was like a chorus.

Then there was silence. It was as if the size and beauty of it took their breath away.

Then the excited talk began again, as each tried to give expression to what he felt.

"So tremendous at this end!"

"And so small over there in New Jersey!"

"No! It only looks that way."

"What is on beyond?"

"Our whole country. Across there—that's west."

"How long does it take to get to the other ocean?"

"A whole week in a car. But not in an airplane!"

"There's an airplane now!"

Then they recalled memories of the bridge at night with its strings of lights and the powerful yellow beam which warned the airplanes of towers and cables.

"But I don't see the lighthouse!" one little girl suddenly exclaimed.

So the teacher led them on down the steep street. Their impulse was to go headlong, pellmell, without restraint, to rush and break loose out of line. They scowled and chafed at being kept in line, at being kept under physical control, when they were intoxicated by this great open expanse of bridge and sky.

At the bottom of the hill, they stopped to look up at the bridge from a very different angle. It looked greater than ever. People seemed so small!

"See the little man walking on the bridge?" a child cried. "Can you really walk across it?"

"But how slowly the cars seem to go!" another marvelled.

"But if you were up there," explained his friend, "they would be going fast!"

There was still another curved street to walk down and around, and then a long flight of steep steps led down to the Drive. As they went along they kept saying, "It's getting bigger! We're getting closer!"

At the bottom of the steps, waiting for a green light so they could cross, they turned and looked back. A towering stone wall stood behind them, built from a great variety of huge rocks.

"Look at that one!" a boy cried out in excitement. "It's just like the mica rock we have in school!"

The whole class shared his joy. There was great excitement about the bridge, the hill, and the wall. There

91

was a feeling that all these things belonged to their city and to them.

The light changed to green and together they crossed to the other side. And there was another stone wall. But it was low and they could see over. At the foot of a woodsy hill with winding paths they saw the river. But still they could not see the little red lighthouse.

The path curved down through grass. The park at last! They all began to talk about picnics and summer.

"Can we eat now?" a dozen voices chirped.

"We're not quite there yet," the teacher said, "but soon!"

There was still a little tunnel to go through which they entered with thundering and echoing shouts, and there ahead framed by its curving dome, was the broad gray river, and above it the Palisades, and the sweeping sky. Then the trail led down rocky slopes to the shore.

"Oh, see the man fishing!" one cried. "On that pointed rock there!"

"That's where the Indians must have fished," another cried.

"Where? Where?" the class was alert.

"Oh, I see an Indian path," cried one. "See! That little path with no cement."

"That's right," answered another. "The sidewalks weren't here then."

"The benches weren't either!" they went on. "Or the bridge."

"Or the lighthouse!"

"Or the stone walls!"

"There's the lighthouse! There!" called one. "Can we go in?" For a moment they had forgotten their lunches.

"It's locked," the teacher had to admit.

"Oh—oh," a little girl called sadly. Then she brightened. "But how does the man get in?" She was thinking of the story. Then she and her friend began playing out a fantasy.

"Keys! Keys!"

"But where is he?"

"It's not night!"

"I have a key!"

"You haven't."

"Yes I have—but it's home!"

"You bring it next time."

"I will!"

"See the bell?"

"Where does the light shine out?"

"Up there! To warn the boats! Sharp rocks here!"

While they played this little game, another group stood discussing the Indians.

"Where are the Indians?" It was as if they ought to find them here now.

"Oh, they live like we do now."

"I know some Indians. They are good Indians."

"But where are their houses?"

"Rotted away. They were made of bark."

"You could dig fishing worms out of this mud."

"Oh, look at that bench made of half a log."

"If we had that in school, we could make a dugout."

"People found arrowheads here. And stone tools. Let's search."

While the children talked they began to open their lunches. Some sat around the picnic tables put there by the Park Department. Others found a nice rock seat, and as they munched their sandwiches, kept up a steady lookout for arrowheads.

"Oh, look here!" cried one boy, running up to the teacher. "Do you think this could be an arrowhead?"

The teacher and child examined it well. They looked for the proper notches on the side. They looked at it from all viewpoints to watch for symmetry. And they had to say no.

But that did not quell the interest. Lunches finished, many kept up the search, while others ran and played in

a grassy space nearby. Although no real arrowheads were found, they gathered a choice collection of beautiful stones, and at last had to be called for the long, hard climb back up to the subway station.

Their legs ached and the children groaned as they climbed up the steep, steep steps, then up the steep hill.

Slowly they moved along past a building which had a very attractive iron fence in front of it.

They were quiet and thoughtful now, and the leader asked, "When did iron come here? Before houses or after?" And when the teacher explained, he was amazed.

"Iron comes from rocks? From rocks they made it? Cooked rocks?"

They had gone a number of steps on up the hill before he could quite take it in. Then he said quite seriously, "That must be hard to make! Take a real hot fire! And the iron melts out of the rock?"

Wonder. Silence. Slow, slow climbing. And after a little more thinking, another question.

"Does all metal come from the ground? All metal? Even that shiny brass railing?"

Again he was lost in silence and wonder.

A city child was relating himself to his world in a new way. And as the class reached the top of the hill and the subway entrance, this boy, turning nine years old, declared,

"When I grow up, I'm going to do hard work. Hard! You get lots of money for a real hard job. . . . I don't want an easy job. . . . I wouldn't mind being a man right now!"

¶ A CLASS, Where there is Plenty

Here is a room with sunny windows across one end, reaching from low cubbies to the ceiling.

But Where Is The Teacher?

As we enter, there is a busy hum of activity with groups of children living dramatically the life of the Manhattan Indians.

In one corner is a wigwam made of heavy paper, painted by the children. In front of it sits Judith, playing Indian mother. She is wearing a costume which she has made herself. Her "baby," bound to a flat board, is propped up beside her, watching her braid corn husks. David, "the father," crouches near a little pile of stones. He is busy trying to tie a pointed stone onto a piece of wood. But where is the teacher?

We look for her where several table-like desks have been pulled together and a group of children are crayoning designs on their own costumes which seem to have been made from worn pajamas dyed tan. The children go over to consult open books which stand on a shelf above a well-stocked bookcase. But the teacher is not there.

Oh, there she is! She has just raised her head. She has been bending over an old trunk full of costume materials. A quiet little girl stands beside her folding lengths of red calico, shirts, and old sheets.

As the teacher raises her head, a boy who had been busy near a big workbench comes up to her with a short length of some kind of hollow stick which he is making into a little flute. He has just finished digging another hole on its side and wants her to stop and listen. He puts the unfinished flute to his lips and trills a strange little tune.

Vera, who is pounding corn in a chopping bowl, stops to listen. So do Judith and David beside their wigwam, and the group working on costumes. A few children who have been writing raise their heads and hold their pencils quiet for a moment. Their faces light up with approval and appreciation. Then the boy moves away and they resume their activities.

We move over to the book shelves and sit down to browse. This seems to be a room where one can be himself, follow his own interests, be comfortable. The labels on the shelves read: Indians, Easy Fiction; Indians, Advanced Fiction; Earth Science, Myths and Legends; Fact Books on Indians; Indian Music; Books on How to Make Things the Indian Way.

As we look up from these shelves we notice other things. There is no "Science Corner," but there are science materials everywhere. The whole room is something of a woodland scene. A great pile of cornstalks stands in one corner, a beautiful bouquet of beach grass in another. Ears of corn hang from several hooks on the wall, gourds are arranged in groups to dry. And one long shelf over the cubbies near the windows holds an attractively arranged collection of stones, bones, shells, supple branches, neat piles of bark. A large sandtable with real earth, growing grass and little trees holds a small accurate model of a woodland Indian village. There are even some tiny clay animals in the scene.

We wonder how long this goes on, and what the next "period" will be. Do these children ever learn arithmetic and spelling? How did all this get started? What *is* the teachers' role?

What Comes Next?

Now the children who were writing are getting together, comparing their papers. They seem to be acting out short scenes. The laughter of the group doing the acting attracts attention, and it is not long before a small audience has gathered, sitting on the floor to watch. Some have brought their work, which they continue. Others just watch.

Now we discover the teacher's role, at least part of it. She comes to hand us a paper on which she has given the children a writing assignment. They were asked to write ideas for scenes in an Indian play.

The one they are acting now is "a big bear beating his little child."

Next comes a fishing scene. Two boys get down on their stomachs at the brink of a make-believe river. They are "Indians fishing with their hands."

At this a number of spectators insist on showing the boys how they would do it and soon a whole line of "Indians" are down at the river's edge grabbing for fish. Their imagination knows no bounds.

The teacher comes over with a big Indian tom-tom, and asks if they would like to be accompanied. Before we know it, the whole group has been swept into a "rhythms" period. They act out "turtles walking by the water," "beavers building dams," "hunters shaping arrowheads of stone." Then the teacher gives each child a turn on the drum to originate any rhythm he likes for the others to dance to. We begin to see the interplay of children's initiative and teacher's guidance.

Building Their Own Norms

Now the children have a good physical workout in dramatic rhythms, leaping like animals, escaping the hunter, creeping through the forest with great control, rowing upstream against the current in their dugout canoes, dragging a great tree trunk down to the water.

"Now," the teacher declares as they are resting, "we need to make some decisions before arithmetic time.

"Vera has written a short play about Henry Hudson and she would like you to hear it to see whether some of you would like to act it out."

Vera reads her play, which is rather meager, and several children suggest things which could be added.

"I'd like to help Vera to write that over again," Robert declares. "There's not enough excitement in it for boys."

Vera looks crestfallen.

"Girls like excitement too, don't you think?" retorts Judith.

"Why not have something in it that everyone likes?" the teacher said.

Vera is getting more courageous. She declares, "Well, this is the part I like. You write your own."

"Sure. O.K. Why not? Then we can add them all together."

"Some hodgepodge that will be," Judith declares again.

"Oh, well, we can smooth it out later. We can fit it together!" Another chimes in.

"At least, that's one way we can all be satisfied," says another.

"That's all the time we have now," the teacher says. "So put away all the materials, and arrange your desks for arithmetic."

"Gee, I'm going to hurry with that today," David calls. "I've already got an idea for the play. Say, Miss Isaacs, may I start working on my part if I finish my arithmetic before the time is up?"

"Arithmetic and," she smiles, "you know what else!"

"Oh, sure. I know, spelling. But I've only got three words that were wrong in my story."

So the teacher does have responsibility for guiding the program! There are times when certain regular schedules are kept. It does not all depend on chance.

Everything At Hand

The children quickly put away the materials they have been working with and pull their desks and chairs into orderly rows. What a strange feeling one gets as this checkerboard effect comes to place in the woodland scene. In a few moments there is not a sound in the room. Concentration on the job at hand seems perfect. The teacher moves quietly from desk to desk as hands go up for help.

During this period of quiet work we have time to notice what we missed before when the children themselves absorbed all of our attention.

There is a sink with running water. There is an electric grill on a fire-proof table. There are cupboards full of bright colored paints. There is a great covered crockery jar full of moist clay.

No wonder the children can develop their ideas so fully and richly with everything at hand.

Harmony with Diversity

We return a few days later to see whether or not the play *did* come together. How could it, when each child went off on his own tangent, his own particular interest, without first making a general plan? This seemed like carrying freedom a little too far. We were inclined to expect, like Judith, quite a "hodgepodge." And how about mental discipline in bending one's thoughts and efforts toward an ordered pattern?

As we enter, we hear great commotion. The woodland is in an uproar.

Let's see what the children are doing now.

"Pile up the desks!" the boys are shouting. "Come on, fellows!" Four boys race across the room, others following. Before we know it they are moving the desks around at top speed.

"Careful, boys! Careful." It is the teacher, and she's warning, "Watch out! Don't crash into one another!"

But the boys seem to have an ordered plan. They arrange some of the desks in a row and put another row on top.

And look who emerges from the wigwam! Henry Hudson himself, tall hat, red jacket, puffed knee breeches and all. Our boys are now on top of the desks crouching and ready with their arrows as Hudson gets into his "scenery boat," and begins to sail up the "river."

This is a far cry from the play we heard Vera read. And what part have the girls made for themselves? The girls are emerging from the wigwam now, carrying clay bowls they have made. Five of them have "babies" on their backs, big rag dolls strapped to their cradle boards. They put the bowls down at the foot of Inwood Hill (that's what the desks are meant to be).

Vera creeps up to speak to the scouts on top of the hill.

"Shall we flee?" she cries in a frightened voice. "Are our little ones in danger?"

"Stay in the wigwam," orders her warrior protector. "The strange ship with wings is passing on. We will keep watch!"

But Little Shrimp, son of Edith—Spanking Mother they call her—escapes from the wigwam and tries to join the brave men on top of the hill. Edith, true to her name, captures him and brings him back, spanking him on the way.

"All down now," calls the teacher. "We'll have to talk about this part before we go on." Reluctantly they come down and all sit on the floor together.

"Well, how about it?" The teacher has to be leader now. The children are too excited.

"One thing," Vera complains, "Edith is carrying this spanking business too far. Indian mothers weren't like that!"

"That's right," chorused several other little girls.

"Some were!" Edith defends herself, "I read a story with a very cross Indian mother in it."

"Well, that's not the kind of Indian mother I want to be," Vera insists.

Everyone laughs.

"And Henry Hudson should kidnap an Indian and take him up the river," David puts in. "That really happened. I can get the book!"

"We'll shoot him for that. We'll get him." It is the big boy of the class who rises now, threatening Henry Hudson who sits among them. Again everybody laughs.

Then David says quite seriously, "But I want to be the Indian boy who has his dream, and finds out which spirit is going to be his elder brother all through life—and—and—I don't see how it can fit in with all this wild part."

"It could come first. That's easy," declares Vera. "A play shouldn't be all wild. And I want to sing an Indian lullaby to my baby in its cradle."

Food For Growth

So it does come together when they work this way. With all their differences and needs, somehow each is finding his place, and there is a place for him.

Here there is room for growth and food for growth. Here there are few occasions for anger, few reasons to step on one another's toes, little feeling of being hemmed in or cramped.

But it is not just the big room and the wonderful materials. It is the teacher's ability to allow for freedom of expression and action and excitement. It is also her ability to control it when it seems about to burst out of bounds.

The teacher is not a commander. She does not stand up in front and "lead" her willing sheep. She is a collaborator in research, a good friend, a playmate, a creative worker herself. But she is also a strong authority when it is necessary.

And she has created the conditions for growth by her choice of materials which can be almost self-teaching, by her preparation and by her determination to keep the creative spirit alive in the middle years.

¶ MARIE, Who Did Not Understand

What They Were Saying

The movable desks in this class were pushed back and a few of the children were bouncing a ball against the blackboard, trying to make it bounce from the floor to a large circle drawn on the board.

One from each side was keeping score.

But a thin, dark-eyed little girl sat apart, shy and unwilling to play.

"Try, Marie," the teacher begged pleasantly. "You can do it."

But Marie ducked her head, and moved it as if to say no.

Although she did not yet know the language, since she had recently arrived from Puerto Rico, the teacher was trying to make her more comfortable by urging her into the game. But evidently Marie was not yet able to be a part of the group, even in a game.

Still More Difficult

"It is still more difficult for her during times when we are reading," the teacher explained to the principal.

"Perhaps not," the principal suggested. "That may be the very place where you can make her feel most comfortable. How about Nilda? She knows both languages well. Perhaps you could work something out with her."

Taking The Class Into Her Confidence

The teacher decided to have a talk with the class and bring Nilda in on some kind of help for Marie.

"How do you think we could make Marie feel more at home, and help her learn English?" she asked.

"We could give her a party." This came from a vivacious girl who looked sideways at Marie as she suggested it. Marie sat now with crayons and paper, but she was not using them. She understood that the teacher was speaking to the children about her English.

"No, I think Marie is too shy for a party," another burst out. "We should start to teach her English right away."

Marie looked puzzled.

"Oh," the teacher said, "I'm afraid Marie thinks we are saying unfriendly things about her English. That is one word she knows. Nilda, tell her in Spanish that we are talking about how to help her. Tell her that we want to be her friends."

Someone Who Understands

Nilda slipped into the seat beside Marie, and the two whispered softly together. The puzzled expression faded and a look of relief, almost a smile, spread over Marie's face.

"I know what we could do," a boy exclaimed, and in a moment he rushed up to the teacher and began talking excitedly in an undertone.

The teacher then explained his idea to the class.

"Paul suggests that we have an interpreter as they do in the United Nations. Nilda could interpret. The class could explain things to Marie and Nilda could translate into Spanish."

Nilda, still with Marie, heard this discussion and her dancing eyes showed that she would love it.

"But what shall we tell her?" asked a big girl in the last row. "What do you suppose she is interested in?"

"Maybe she could ask us things," a boy suggested, "about what we do in the room. Maybe about New York!"

"I'll ask her," Nilda said, and again the heads were together whispering.

"She doesn't know what to ask," Nilda said finally.

"Then let's ask her!" It came like a chorus.

"All right," the teacher agreed. "Who will begin?"

The boy stood up, went over in front of the two girls, and said, "How did you come to New York?"

Again there were whispers as Nilda interpreted and got an answer.

"Boat." She translated to the class.

Now hands were waving. Everyone had an idea.

"Ask her how big is her island?" was the next question. But Marie shook her head.

"We ought to get out the map, and see if she can find it," said one.

"No, that's too hard," another objected thoughtfully.

"Ask her what she eats in Puerto Rico." This came from a girl.

Soon the answer came back.

"Beans and rice."

"Gee, is that all?" exclaimed a boy.

"Maybe we should stop now and try it another time," the teacher suggested. "We don't want to get too personal. Try to think up some more ideas for tomorrow, and write them down. But we have made a good beginning."

From the pleased expression on Marie's face they could tell they *had* made a good start.

Children Have Good Ideas

Next day the teacher wrote a list of all the suggestions the children had brought. Here they are:

Invite all the Spanish-speaking children in the school to a party, and serve some kind of Spanish food, and have them sing Spanish songs.

Take a trip to the dock to see the boat on which Marie came to New York.

Take Marie on a trip to the top of a tall building so she can see the harbor where her ship came in.

Make a table map, and a little toy boat coming from Puerto Rico to New York.

Take a trip to a store where they sell Spanish foods, and have Marie tell their names and let Nilda interpret.

Help Marie make an easy reader for herself, with Spanish words on one side and English on the other. She could tell about her home and her school on the island, and draw pictures, and we could help her print it.

Get some sugar cane, and learn about it.

What Was In Store For The Class

In the beginning and without communication, how could the children know what was in this quiet little girl's mind and feelings? They could not guess how she missed her own little house, poor as it was, where she sat outside under the stars with her grandfather who told her stories. They could not know about the tall upright pole he had stuck in the ground and the little birdhouse on top of it, or how the tiny canary who came there sang to her all through the day. They could know nothing of the big steamers that sailed before her eyes every day, or the tired, sad look of her father when he came home from the long, hard day in the cigar factory. Or of the tiny gardens where they could raise their own sweet potatoes.

Without communication they could know none of this. Yet now, in helping Marie to feel at home, the class had in store for it a rich experience!

From One Island to Another

The teacher, too, had visions of things to do which would make Marie important to the class, and make her former home real to them. She would do what Columbus had done when Queen Isabella asked him to report on the island. She would crumple up a piece of paper and throw it on the table before her, and say in Columbus' own words, "It is an island full of mountains and valleys." And she would bring in samples of coffee, cedar, palm, ebony, bamboo, sweet potatoes, bananas, cocoa and nuts which would bring Marie's memories flooding back, which would loosen her tongue, and help her communicate about her own life, the only one she knew, the one where all her feelings were centered.

And then the teacher would help her to know this new island, its beauties as well as its heartaches. Perhaps the time would come when Marie's mother could come to the class, and show how she made beautiful embroidered linen. And Marie's big brother, an expert at straw hat weaving, might teach them a little of his craft and skill. Then the soft-spoken, shy child would become gay and full of songs as she became herself.

No Limit

In helping Marie they would all develop a deeper interest in the language and feelings not only of a little Puerto Rican girl, but of other foreign children perhaps right in their own class. Other mothers might come too, with their memories, their crafts, and their stories from the lands where they were born. Marie and the others would then come to know more about America, and how it was a land of many, many peoples, all coming here to live together, each people remembering the place of its birth, bringing its songs and stories, but all becoming a new people in a new world.

¶ FRANK, Walking Encyclopedia

Small Boy With Big Words

"He never stops talking. But he hasn't got a friend in the world. That boy knows *too* much." This is what the teacher said of Frank.

The class came in out of a snow storm one day and began talking about their exciting experiences with the storm, and also relating news they had heard over the radio.

Frank asked for a turn to speak.

But what was he saying? It was a fast jumble with many big words coming through. Troposphere, stratosphere, ionosphere, polar front, barometer. The rest of the class was impatient.

"Jimmy wants to speak now," the teacher interrupted.

But Frank went right on, even a little faster if that were possible. The teacher tried to find another place to break in. But there seemed to be a breathless hurry in Frank's talk.

"Thank you, Frank," the teacher said firmly and with finality. "Now Jimmy."

Jimmy looked at Frank uncertainly, wondering how to start. This had happened before. When Frank got going, what was the use?

But Frank dropped exhausted into his seat. At last someone else could be heard.

In The Yard

The storm over, the class went down to the yard. They were first to play in the untrampled snow. But it was not untrampled for long. One of the girls began to run round and round in a big circle, crying, "Fox and Geese. Fox and Geese," while the boys made great speed building up forts and pelting one another with snow.

All except Frank. He stood near the teacher pointing out a wire all covered with thick ice, and giving her a scientific explanation.

After she had listened a while, she suggested, "Don't you want to play? Everyone is having so much fun."

"No, I don't think so," Frank drawled in his little old man way, which he seemed to use whenever he felt threatened. "I don't really think I'd care to." Then, catching sight of a truck, he began another long explanation.

"That's a Borden's truck from that pasteurizing plant by the river," he began. And again the teacher felt trapped, pinned down. She had to listen.

"What can be done about this child?" she thought to herself. "No wonder the children don't like him."

He Never Even Picks Up A Crayon

Back in the classroom the children were having a short free period for drawing or quiet games. Many of them were at work on snow pictures, using quantities of white

chalk. Some made pictures of themselves on skates or sleds. A few drew igloos and Eskimo catching seal.

But Frank was trying to entice two girls away from their drawing. He was trying to explain to them a weather map he had brought that morning.

"Oh, leave us alone," one girl said. "We don't care." Some boys overheard the complaint, and said, "There he goes again!"

It was not that they disliked talk. They liked to talk, too. but this was not really communication. It was just being flooded with words. In fact, they thought of him not as a person but as a book! One of the mothers had told the teacher her daughter had asked the distance of the earth from the sun. "I don't remember," the mother had said, "but I'll look it up."

"Oh, never mind," the girl had said, "Frank will know."

Not What It Seemed

But this teacher felt there must be a way to help Frank. If she could get him interested in working with his hands, perhaps he could demonstrate a science experiment to the class. She would try to follow up his interest in the ice on the wire.

She checked out a book of simple experiments from the school library. It would be fine if Frank could be induced to work out an experiment with a few of the other boys.

"Frank," she suggested, "how about doing an experiment for the group? There are some good suggestions in this book on freezing."

Frank was interested. He took the book eagerly and sat down to leaf through it. Several of the boys crowded around. They began to make suggestions, to point impulsively to illustrations.

Frank looked up, startled. He looked for an opening—a place to break out through the surrounding group. Then as if that were impossible, he buried his face in the book and shut the other children out. But only for a moment. He suddenly threw the book on the desk and pushed his way through.

"May I go and get a drink?" he asked breathlessly.

And the teacher let him go.

When he returned, he said he did not really care for that book. The experiments were too simple.

But the teacher had seen his panic. He was afraid of being drawn in to work with others. He had to keep a safe distance. It became clear to her that she was expecting too much too soon. She would have to start by letting him try an experiment entirely by himself. Maybe in time she could find a way to help him work with other children.

But she was not sorry for this little incident. It had revealed a good deal to her. She would go ahead trying out other ideas too, for she knew that it was only through concrete steps like these that she could come to understand her problem with Frank.

She began planning these next steps. She would try to get Frank interested in writing as well as talking—writing stories and reports. Perhaps eventually he could be drawn in to help the class with some kind of class paper. Maybe she could give him responsibilities in connection with the library.

She knew, of course, that a teacher sometimes has to call in other help in the end, no matter how imaginative she may be. This difficulty of Frank's might be one that only a trained psychologist could resolve. It was easy to see that the boy was not really happy.

Meanwhile, she would take her concrete steps in the classroom. It remained to be seen what she could accomplish.

¶ EVELYN, Always Sulking

It was autumn. In this fourth grade room, all but filled with stationary desks, the children were studying Dutch farm life on old Manhattan.

Two large stretches of brown wrapping paper were attached to the wall in different places, backdrops for a play the children were planning.

The room was quietly buzzing as the children moved freely from sketching at their desks to consult with the teacher or with committee chairmen before taking chalk and adding their contribution to the general scene. The group had evidently made careful plans, since the blackboard was covered with suggestions for each scene. One scene was a huge fireplace with Dutch tiles and surrounding utensils. The other was a farm with a house and barn, a field, garden, orchard, and domestic animals.

In all this variety there was surely some little part each child could draw, if it were only to paint peaches and apples on the trees in the orchard.

If this were so, then how explain the overgrown girl sulking in the corner, her shoulders hunched over, her back turned to the happy activity? It seemed she would have none of it.

The Cheerful Approach

Evidently the teacher was anxious to have Evelyn participate. She worked her way through the busy group to Evelyn.

"Come on, Evelyn," she urged cheerfully. "I'm sure you can draw. Why don't you try?"

Evelyn brushed a wisp of blonde hair from her eyes but she did not answer. Her chin only became more stubborn, her lips more pouting. Beatrice, working away at her desk on a sketch for a Dutch tile, spoke out roughly, "Oh, you never want to do anything."

Evelyn flung herself away from both the child and teacher.

"Oh, that's not true," the teacher declared, trying to make up for the discouraging remark. "You just look at the blackboard, Evelyn, and you'll get an idea." She walked away, but not before giving Beatrice a warning shake of her head.

The work went on, but Evelyn did not participate. Instead she took a fairy tale book from the shelf and pored over the pictures.

Stimulating The Imagination

On another day, the teacher tried something else. Perhaps what was good for the class would be good for Evelyn. Perhaps it was just her dull, drab life at home that made it impossible for her to get enthusiastic about a kind of life she had never known. The teacher looked up an amusing old journal, a diary written by two men who came visiting the island of Manhattan. It was full of descriptions of being entertained and fed in the old Dutch homes, with oysters roasting on the blazing fire of oak and hickory. There were nuts and berries and corn too, and roast venison and wild turkey and wild goose. Even watermelons were grown in what is now Brooklyn. And hogs gobbled up the piles of peaches that dropped, overripe, from heavily laden branches.

The teacher read aloud to the class and there was much laughter and chuckling as the children imagined the life that had once been here where now the rich land is weighed down with tremendous stone and concrete buildings.

Some of the children had asked to sketch while the teacher read. But they were listening, along with the others. Only Evelyn was absorbed in her fairy tale book.

What Are Evelyn's Real Feelings?

The teacher wondered. Did Evelyn want to participate? Or was she really not interested?

She worried a little too. Evelyn was the only child in the class with whom she had no real relationship. Yet she was aware that a teacher cannot always meet the needs of every child. Sometimes it is best to get another person in on it. Certain personalities clicked. Others didn't. There was little you could do about it.

She talked it over with the teacher next door, and invited her in to observe.

"She is unattractive," the other teacher noticed. "It's probably something much deeper than just being afraid to try to draw. She seems to be trying to make herself unnoticed."

They talked again, and the teacher next door invited Evelyn in to her room to help her mix paints. Then she visited Evelyn's class when they were working on their murals again.

Evelyn stood watching the others, leaning against the wall. She was still sulking. When the visiting teacher came up and asked Evelyn what part she was going to draw, Beatrice broke in again, "Oh, don't pay any attention to her. She's in a bad mood!"

"Maybe she has a reason for feeling that way," was the visitor's answer. And as she said it, she smiled at Evelyn, as if to tell her she was trying to help.

"I can guess how you feel," the teacher went on.

"Sometimes when I try to write a story, and I don't like what I have written, I feel the same way. Maybe even worse. I get so angry, I tear it up into little bits."

Evelyn looked at the teacher. Her face lost the scowl. She looked at the children drawing and painting. Then she went hesitantly for crayons and paper.

She came back and sat down by the visiting teacher. "You show me," she begged, with a wistful smile.

The Same Thing May Not Work Twice

No one could know just what had happened inside Evelyn. A moment before she was stolid and sour. Now she was trying to draw a peach so that it would look round and ripe and rosy.

The regular teacher could not believe her eyes. She could not help feeling just a twinge of jealousy. Why couldn't *she* have found the secret to unlocking this child's feelings? Yet she was proud that she had helped to bring this about.

But the visiting teacher knew in a way what had made the difference. She had shown the child that she was human herself. She had admitted that teachers, too, have to struggle with problems, with their own angry feelings, sometimes with defeat. She had shared her own creative problems with Evelyn. And it had made Evelyn know she was not alone. She was not the only one who might be discouraged with herself. Here was a teacher, a grownup, willing to admit it.

Still it might not have worked with another child.

Later when the two teachers talked it over together, they decided that in some ways children and adults have the same kinds of troubles. It is only a difference of degree. Where there is no need to feel superior or "perfect," where there is security enough to receive help that is offered, then creative impulses can be released, often beyond all imagination.

¶ PETER, Who Forgot What
He Meant To Say

The class was not in the habit of thinking together. They had been trained to stand up and recite, giving back what they had read in a book. But this teacher was trying out something new.

She was trying to help the children learn how to think —to think on their feet, out loud—and to respect each other's contributions. She wanted to encourage the slightest attempt, however feeble, and to make each child feel that what he had to say was of value. She hoped that the children would gradually accept her attitude and make it their own, but she knew how easily the capacity to think could be killed by disapproval, by fear of ridicule, by condemnation.

The children were much concerned about the water shortage in the city and reminded each other often not to waste water. Yet they had only a vague concept of the source of the pure cold water that rushes out of city faucets—water that can make the difference between health and illness for millions of people.

So this teacher was trying to draw the children out, to bring to life in every child's memory country experiences with water, so that a foundation and interest could be established for further study of the city's water problems.

"Has anyone ever taken a drink from a nice cold spring in the country?" she asked.

Surprisingly enough, in this congested city neighborhood, two or three hands went up. She called on one boy who told of his life in the South. He told it so vividly that everyone was attentive. It began to remind others of their experiences and soon a number of hands were waving.

118

The teacher called on Peter, who was sitting quietly.

Peter rose to speak, but nothing happened. When the others saw him hesitate they became impatient. Hands were waving all over the room. Peter looked around and saw the hands. He tried to begin, but stumbled a little, and someone laughed.

Peter could not get started. His face turned red, and the whole class began to titter. His head dropped in shame and he looked as though he would like to sink through the floor.

"Just a minute," the teacher said quietly, but seriously. "I want the class to try an experiment."

Fortunately they were intrigued, wondering what she meant. They were ready to listen.

"What happened to Peter," she said, "could happen to anyone. Even when you know something quite well, if someone is trying to beat you to it, it is easy to forget. When you wave your hands in the air it prevents Peter from thinking. Let's try just the opposite and see if it works."

The class responded and Peter tried again. He spoke slowly and sometimes groped for words. But he told a good story. It was about a camp experience when a rainstorm had clogged up the brook with sticks and leaves, and the children had to go in bathing suits to clean it out before they could have the faucets working in their wash house again.

The class felt noble and Peter felt relieved. As time went on, the teacher noticed Peter more and more. The children often teased him, and he seemed to expect to be attacked. He seemed almost to invite teasing. What was it that made Peter so vulnerable?

A Partial Answer

One day Peter's father came for him in the car, and the teacher was waiting on the sidewalk ready to rush downtown. She gratefully accepted the lift to the subway which Peter's father offered her.

"Well, what did you learn today, Peter?" the father asked, giving the teacher a wink.

"We—we—" Peter began.

"Go on, go on," the father broke in.

"We—we learned," Peter continued, "about the Keno —no, that's not it—the Kenico Dam."

"Oh, Kensico!" the father chimed in. "Kensico—can't you say it? That's not a hard word."

It was his tone, more than what he said that made the teacher cringe. She tried to change the subject, but the father would not be turned away from his purpose.

"He'll know how to pronounce it tomorrow," he declared. "You check up on it."

But her heart only sank a little further. She was glad when they arrived at the subway and she could escape. Now, what to do about Peter?

The Teacher's Responsibility

Correct pronunciation was important, certainly. But the father's pressure was getting just the opposite result from the one he sought. And it was making Peter insecure as well.

Could she do anything? Of one thing she was certain. She could refrain from putting pressure on Peter in school, such as she saw his father putting on. Perhaps she had not been helping Peter any by asking him to get up and speak before the class when it was so hard for him. She would have to find opportunities for him to talk slowly at his own rate, with just one or two children at a time. She would have to make an extra effort to see that successes came his way.

It would not be easy to accomplish results, she knew. A father's influence can far outweigh that of a teacher. Yet she was sure that it would be worthwhile for her to do what she could. Certainly Peter's problem would only be aggravated if both teacher and father were putting on too many pressures. And perhaps in time she could get Peter's father to see her point.

There was nothing wrong with Peter. There was only something wrong with Peter's world.

¶ CARL, Who Had to Get Even

All morning Carl had been sticking his foot into the aisle every time a girl went up to sharpen her pencil. All morning he had nothing but sharp retorts for anyone who spoke to him.

But now after being completely absorbed in drawing comic book characters during free time, Carl is soft and affable, almost tender in his attitude toward the others. He still sits with a classmate, and their arms are around each other's shoulders. What is the subterranean power of these comics which often seem so evil to adults, yet which have such a satisfying and relaxing effect on children's troubled spirits?

Trying To Help Carl

The teacher feels a little guilty in letting him draw these things in school at all, and is eager to find what she thinks might be a more constructive solution. She tries putting Carl in charge of milk and cookies which the children buy each day. Perhaps this will make him feel important, and ease some of his tension. Let's see how he reacts to this situation.

He sits at the teacher's desk now with the box of cookies and the row of milk cartons before him. As each child comes up, Carl puts his money in a little box and gives him change, marking a record of the sale on a sheet of paper. Here comes Jim, a fat boy, holding out two pennies. Carl watches to see that he takes only two cookies, and then before marking it down he suddenly jibes, "Anybody as fat as you ought to go on a diet!"

Jim flushes, but does not answer back. Carl chews his pencil nervously and finally marks down the amount.

For the girl in braids and bright ribbons dancing up the aisle he has a different quip, "Do you have to prance around like an actress every time you get milk?"

"So what!" she flings back, putting on more of an act than ever.

Carl is certainly full of nettles.

Does Anything Work?

The teacher makes other attempts. But when she puts him in charge of scenery, he orders the children about and they refuse to paint any more. When he is the "caller" in the game of Giant Steps, he takes his irritation out on smaller children, forcing them to take only "half of a baby step." And each time he punishes one of his classmates, in one way or another, his face twitches, or he chews his fingernails, or his pencil. Certainly some very strong feelings are bottled up here and popping out all the time. He seems to have to get even with the whole world.

In The Museum

We follow Carl at the end of the line, as the class trails through the Dinosaur room in the museum. He suddenly grabs the arm of the boy next to him.

"Hey, Bill," he says in an excited tone, "Look at that turtle. Why, he could pick you up with his little pinky!"

And, "By Golly!" This ejaculation bursts out as he leans his head far back to grasp the tremendous size of a towering skeleton.

"Gee," he continues, still holding Bill and gazing up, although the rest of the class have gone on far ahead.

"Gee, Bill, you couldn't get away from that guy no matter how big a tree you'd climb. He could nip you right off with his front teeth!"

This reminds us of some little fellows in the kindergarten, boasting about what their fathers could do to the other little fellow's father. We get a little new light on Carl, and wonder if there is something here which is related to the comics with their supermen and daredevils.

It Helps To Keep A Few Notes

This teacher is taking a course in child development, and she has been keeping a few notes on Carl to discuss with her own teacher. She finds that the notes on Carl begin to form a pattern, but she is not sure just what they mean. She decides to have a conference with Carl's mother before discussing this as a case study in the adult class.

In talking with Carl's mother, the teacher does not discuss her notes. But she does mention his general irritability. She shows how it is slowing up Carl's work and how it affects the work of the class. She assures the mother that she does not consider this a fault in Carl but an indication that something rather serious is bothering him. Perhaps mother and teacher together can find out what it is and help him.

Finally the story comes out that Carl has a younger brother who in every way is more alert and charming. He always gets all the attention from friends and strangers. As a matter of fact, even the parents find the younger boy easier to live with than Carl ever was.

This throws a great deal of light on Carl's irritation at school. The teacher suggests that even though the parents are not partial to the younger boy, Carl may feel that they are. In order to reassure him, it might be wise to make very special plans for a while. Perhaps the father might take Carl on special excursions at times when the younger boy was being entertained at the home of a friend. It would be worth trying. Little changes like that often worked miracles in a child's feelings. It would help to clear up any doubts he might have about himself.

The teacher promised that she too would help. She would talk to the assistant principal at school and see if he could give Carl a little special attention.

In The Class On Child Development

Carl's problem is a typical one and nothing the teacher had to say was a breach of confidence.

After the teacher had read her notes to the class, the psychologist first asked members of the class to give their interpretations, and asked them to try to remember similar behavior in children they had known.

"It is obvious his brother's outstanding popularity has made Carl feel small and worthless in comparison," one teacher said.

"But if he feels secure in his parent's affection, it shouldn't make that much difference," objected another.

"There's nothing you can do about that!" one said. "The problem is what to do in school!"

There were other comments and then the psychologist

made her own suggestions, warning that until the teacher knew more, everything must be taken very tentatively.

"It is possible," the psychologist said, "that on the surface Carl seems to feel toward his brother as his parents and their friends do. But if he has doubts about his own place in the home, there is bound to be a great deal of resentment, not only toward his brother, but toward his parents as well. So long as he can do nothing to change these conditions, he would have to take some of this resentment out on others."

"How about his absorption with the comics?" the teacher asked.

"If they have a soothing effect, there must be a good reason," the psychologist replied. "Perhaps the boy can identify with some of the daredevils and get rid of some of his feelings against his brother in an imaginative, harmless way."

"Wasn't that what he was doing when he talked about the dinosaur picking Bill out of the tree?"

"It might be," the psychologist went on, "but we can't jump to quick conclusions."

The teacher wanted suggestions for a definite plan of attack.

"First of all, you have already done a great deal just by your interest and attitude," the psychologist answered. "You are not blaming the boy too much. You are trying to help. Your talk with his mother should bring results. If it does not, you can go into it with her a little more fully. Tell her some of the things we have talked over here. That may help her to see Carl in a new light. And if she is being too hard on him at home, it may help her to ease up a little on him there."

Well, the teacher had made a beginning. No human problems can be solved overnight. And it was very good to be able to talk them over with others, and to find that she was not the only one who had such problems to face. It was a good feeling. And she felt she was growing, too. It was no mean undertaking, being a teacher.

¶ JOHN, Weaving The Pattern
Of His World

You look over the shoulder of this boy who is completely absorbed in drawing strange designs on a nine by twelve piece of paper. These designs look like long, well-chewed bones. One is like the outline of a primitive tool, others like long islands with curly shores, and the big one in the center is most interesting of all, resembling a real land mass with several points and peninsulas of different shapes and sizes. John is so deep in his thoughts that he does not even know you are standing behind him watching until he has finished and looks up.

What Does It Mean?

What can it mean? You wonder, but do not ask. Perhaps he could not tell you and it would be only intruding, preventing further development, so you go down the aisle and look at the drawings of the other children. After a while you manage to stroll by John's desk again. Now it is perfectly clear. He has named everything. Here on this nine by twelve piece of paper is John's world. He was putting all the pieces together like a puzzle, making them fit. Making them belong to each other in an harmonious whole.

The long "island" on the edge is named ATLANTIC OCEAN. In the upper right-hand corner is NORTH POLE. And at the opposite corner SOUTH POLE. The center of the "primitive tool" is a group: NEW YORK, UNITED STATES, NEW HAMPSHIRE, and at one tip of the same "tool" is MANHATTAN, at the other, THE BRONX. There are many more: BRIDGEPORT, PORTCHESTER, HACKENSACK, WASHINGTON, RICHMOND, AFRICA, CHINA, BRAZIL, TEXAS CITY.

Only Geography?

Is this only geography? Or is it something much deeper and more personal? What has this to do with John's development as a human being? As a growing nine-year-old?

Next day when there is time and the other children are absorbed in work they can do without help, you call John to your desk and ask,

"John, would you mind telling me more about your map?"

John is pleased and goes to get it, sits on a chair by the desk and allows you to write down what he says about each place.

North Pole: "Eskimos live up there."

Bronx: "My father used to live there. It has a park and trees."

New York: "I like New York a lot. I like to go in the Empire State Building. The Chrysler cars that drive around, they come from the Chrysler Building."

United States: "It's a big country. And a proud country. It's brave."

Manhattan: "I think Manhattan is in New York. There is a Manhattan Bridge."

Portchester: "I used to live there. We had picnics and everything. And the children were very nice. We bought balloons."

Bridgeport: "I went up to Bridgeport yesterday. It's something like the country. You play in the grass and everything. And I like the way my aunt cooks."

Washington: "One of my friends went to Washington. She has a house in the woods. And she saw the White House and everything. She didn't go in it though."

Richmond: "Richard told me about Richmond. I think he knows."

127

Hackensack: "My uncle is in Hackensack. I go up there to play with my cousin. We have lots of fun. I told my uncle that the Indians named it, and he said, 'How did you know?' And I told him we were studying about Indians and a lady told us."

Africa: "We saw movies about Africa upstairs. And I copied the name of Africa out of a book. The movies showed elephants, and people carrying things on their heads."

Texas City: "That's where the cowboys live."

Brazil: "Something like Mexico."

China: "In the old days when this country wasn't here, why China was rich but now they're poor because of the war. I read a story about a Chinese Emperor."

South Pole: "Very cold up there. I hope I don't go up there. Don't want to freeze."

New Hampshire: "It's some center of New York, but I think it's out of town."

John's Nine-Year-Old Needs

What does this show about John? This effort of his on his own initiative to relate the elements of his world to one another? What does it show, not just about his vague and sometimes distorted concepts, but about his feelings, his strivings, his fears?

He is impressed by bigness, the big buildings, the fine cars, the big and brave qualities of his country. He has a good family life, affectionate relatives, and he loves the country. He has good memories of picnics and playing in the grass, and the beauty of the sea. And he is trying to take in wider horizons, different ways of living, and serious problems of poverty and war. Everything is said seriously and with feeling. John is trying to relate himself to his world.

What About The Teacher?

This teacher is interested in John as a human being. She is not only concerned about what facts he knows, but also she is interested in his feelings, his wishes, his desire to think for himself, his initiative. Her first consideration is to know John. So she does not laugh or make fun of his misinformation or clumsy expression. Compared with what is going on in his mind and heart, these things are temporarily unimportant. They can be corrected later when he does not know the information is directed at him. To hurt his feelings now would only destroy her relationship with him, and he might not be willing to let her in on his thoughts at all. He might simply close up like a clam and from then on, do his thinking without her.

How Can This Teacher Help To Meet John's Needs?

John wants to know his world, to be related to it, to be related to the people in it who are different, as well as to his familiar uncles and aunts. He wants to know more about the life of the people in Africa who carry burdens on their heads and about the Chinese who "were rich but now are poor."

How can the teacher best satisfy these strivings to understand? How can she help John's world to become even more real?

The great city in which he feels at home and which he "likes a lot" holds the answer. Here he can know children whose parents came from that larger world. He does not have to depend on dry facts which are found in books, for every neighborhood holds life and much of this rich life reflects other parts of the world.

The larger world John is trying to fathom is real through real people. He is striving to relate himself to real people through stories, through what he reads, and through the pictures he sees in the newspaper. Faraway places have meaning only because people live there. He feels with these people in terms of their enjoyment of grass, the sea, picnics, gaiety, war, poverty, all of which he too has experienced.

John's New Friends

Now we see John and his class, after preliminary letters and arrangements, visiting the fourth grade classroom of a school which is mainly Chinese-American.

As the children file into the room, each is told to look up and down the aisles and find the letter he wrote to a member of the class, and then to sit with him.

Thirty children in seats are looking over thirty children walking slowly up and down, wondering which child belongs to the name on his desk. One by one they find their partners, and each seat has two instead of one. At once the Chinese-American children begin to carry out their plans.

John's friend answers in very good English the questions John had written in his letter, then teaches him to write a few words in Chinese. And as John sits there beside a child whose father was born across the sea, he gains a new personal dimension in terms of a foreign land, and a reality almost as clear as that which concerned his aunt whose friend lived near the Atlantic Ocean, or his friend who lived in the woods near Washington and saw the White House but didn't go in.

After John and his Chinese-American friend have

talked together, various children entertain with poems in both Chinese and English, with songs, and with a dragon dance. New, rich, human relations and knowledge and beauty are being woven into John's world.

By VIRGINIA SCHONBORG:

Prologue

Fifth and Sixth Grade Children

And so they grow. . . . Now our children are ten, eleven, twelve. Are they very different from the younger ones? They often seem to be. They're so much bigger, and usually more independent. Sometimes they seem harder to teach!

Of course there are many real differences. The "why's" and "how's" of these children cover the whole world; horizons are farther and broader. Children of this level of maturity no longer think that New Hampshire is in New York. They know a good deal about what other countries are like, and their questions take them even to other planets. Nothing seems too remote "to find out about." Though learning goes on most effectively, as before, through use of experience and first-hand investigation, these children are now able to use a wide variety of source materials to very good advantage. They are acquiring a growing ability to go to books for information, to use maps, picture files, and other sources.

Books alone, however, are not enough for real learnings. Even these seemingly mature children need to make concrete the long-ago and far-away, and to become *involved* with what they are learning, through opportunities to express in their own way some of the information gathered from their source materials. Very often, the more mature among these upper grade children look to language in a new way as a form of expression. In individual writing and in group writing of a play, these children have a new interest in language as craftsmen that extends from grammar, paragraphing and such formal techniques to the subtler techniques of language as an art; the structure or pattern of the whole, effective beginnings and endings, the way to get emphasis and balance. The original plays written by children of these ages often reveal also the development of their *values* or ethical standards, which is rare in younger children. And dramatization further helps them to feel some identification with the Good and Great, which is often a strong need at this stage of growth.

They are eager for group activities which have a peculiar significance to them as they approach adolescence with increased sense of self in relation to other people and to future jobs. They long for recognition by their peers, and get satisfactions in social interchange on a new level. Also they are more willing now to subordinate individual achievement to the achievement of the group. They are ready to write their own class plays, put out their own newspapers, work on group paintings which are more group-organized than those of younger children. They are ready to take museum trips with the class. They are ready to use new skills for acquiring information and content, and to develop through plays, newspapers, dioramas and paintings, a creative use of this content.

Not all of the children, however, are equally ready for these activities. Some of them are afraid to try anything new, perhaps because of so little success in the past. Some have not found any very satisfactory channels to direct their interests into, and lacking this direction cannot make use of what they are learning; some need the learning of "getting along," the ways of getting along with the group more than anything else.

Indeed, there is likely to be very uneven development among children of these grades. On different levels or to different degrees, all of them continue to have needs that run through all ages. Some of these are: need to belong to a group; feeling for fair play which the older children call "justice"; need for constructive and creative activities; interest in information; need for respect, affection, for belonging.

There are some clues to other needs and impulses that first appear or develop greatly among these middle-years and pre-adolescent children—signposts for growth, we can call them—that teachers can use as guides for themselves, as they work to help all of these children find their own ways of learning and achieving. Important among these are:

The need to feel grown up which makes them chafe about their position as children;

The need to become as capable, as knowing, as adequate as possible;

Greatly increased ability to think abstractly which makes it possible for some of these children to comprehend complex relationships;

An attempt to develop a system of values, often shown by a sudden expansion of interests: as, for example, the expansion of interest in how things and people work to include interest in the conditions under which the worker works and what this means to him and his family;

The fact that this early stage of constructing a code of values is deeply influenced not only by the code of children's families but also by the code of their teachers.

Children in these middle years look to us, their teachers, to help them fulfill their needs and direct their impulses. If we can help them find "ways of getting along" through mastery of skills and techniques, if we can help them achieve successful status as members of the group, if we can help them toward constructing a sound code of values, we are helping them in the most important areas of their growing up.

¶ A TIME TO PAINT

It Might Have Been This Way

"Paul, you draw very well, but somehow when you paint you spoil it." Paul looked at his teacher with a worried frown. The rest of the class listened with little interest.

The project was a class painting which would enable the children to pull together and make real use of the information they had been collecting on ways of living in pioneer days in America.

A rather tentative hand went up towards the back of the room.

"Yes, Ralph?"

"I'd like to draw one of the pioneers with a raccoon hat and leggings made out of deer skin and maybe a long gun and some trees and . . ."

"All right, Ralph, all right!" said Miss Peterson. "Now stop your gabbling. Some of you children are so unruly I don't see how you can do anything like a class project. You haven't learned to work alone yet."

Let's look at the class a little more closely. Paul is a boy who can draw, but really does seem to be afraid to paint; Ralph is the child who talks all the time, finishes very little work, but abounds with ideas; over there in the corner is Maria who squirms all day long; and Teresa sitting up straight in the first seat, Teresa who quarrels with everyone and is ready to fight if someone accidentally knocks a pencil or paper from her desk. These are just a few. You have surely seen them before, in your own classrooms. Some of these children have problems so deeply rooted that we as teachers feel we can do very little without special help. However, in front of us sit thirty or forty children. Something can be done.

Suppose Miss Peterson tried to use the class painting project as a group learning situation, as well as a chance for the fifth grade children to work individually at a creative activity. Could this help Ralph and his talking? Could it help Paul who is afraid? Maria who nervously twists all day? Fighting Teresa? Let's shift the scene.

Working Another Way

"Maria," said Miss Peterson, "please get the small yellow paper and give one sheet to each child, and then will you ask someone to help you Scotch-tape the big paper to the bulletin board?" Maria looks surprised but gets up to start the job.

A furiously waving arm goes up in the back of the room. It doesn't seem possible that it can stay attached

to the stocky body of the ten-year-old boy it belongs to. Finally the voice is raised, as well as the arm.

"Miss Peterson, Miss Peterson!"

"Ralph, can't you wait until I'm through talking?"

"Miss Peterson, I have an idea. I want to draw one of those pioneers with a raccoon hat and leggings made out of deer skin and maybe a long gun and some trees . . ."

"Miss Peterson, he's taking all my ideas. He's a pig, Miss Peterson!" cries out Teresa, glaring at Ralph.

"I'm not a pig, you dope! You just haven't got any ideas!"

"Ralph," said Miss Peterson, "remember when we discussed how much space we had for our painting?"

"Yes, I remember."

"I think we said twelve painters, didn't we?" asked Miss Peterson.

"Yes, twelve of us."

"Then perhaps you could make a list right now of the names of the painters and . . ."

"And write down opposite exactly what each person wants to paint!" finished Teresa with a glare at Ralph.

"That's fine, Teresa. Now you get the names down, Ralph, and while you're doing it, all you painters go over in your minds the things we discussed in Social Studies this morning and see if you can decide what you would like to put in this painting."

"How's it going to hang together? Maybe it will all be just spots, spots of people, spots of sod-houses, spots of buffaloes," said Ralph, stopping his writing.

"Oh, Ralph, we'll decide that after we see what we've got," said Paul.

Ralph looked at him a minute, smiled, and said, "O.K."

Miss Peterson said O.K., too, under her breath. Then as the children were writing down their ideas for the painting, she called Paul to her.

"Paul," she said, "would you get the paint out and put the jars in three boxes under the bulletin board?"

Just as she finished, Maria came up and asked Paul to help her with putting up the painting paper.

As she went off, Miss Peterson noticed Paul carrying his sharpened pencil with him.

"Paul, today we'll sketch in with chalk, and some of us will paint, but this is going to be too big a painting for a pencil, isn't it? How about trying the chalk, or the paint?"

"Maybe I'll try," said Paul.

"Miss Peterson, why don't you help me? You're always helping someone else!" Teresa broke in. Miss Peterson looked at angry Teresa standing at her desk. What in the world could make this child so angry all the time? But wait—is it just anger? Aren't those tears in Teresa's eyes? Miss Peterson decided not to say what was on the tip of her tongue. Instead she walked over to Teresa and said, "Of course I want to help you, but really, Teresa, I just haven't had time to get to you yet. I have a good idea for you. Do you remember that story, *The Matchlock Gun*, that we read last month?"

"Yes I do, and I didn't like it much except when the boy gets the gun to protect the family."

"Well, I wonder if we could gather a collection of the books we've read that have helped us in our Social Studies. How about going to the library for some of them? Then when we have them all together you might set them up on the table and we'll think how they might help us with our class painting."

"You mean give us some more ideas?"

"Yes, you might get some ideas to tell the class after you've set up the display, Teresa. I remember that good report you did on fire making and food in pioneer times."

"All right, I'll start with books on the shelf in the room. I remember *Tree-on-the-Trail*. It was good for covered wagons. But I'll get a chance to paint too, won't I?"

"Of course you will, Teresa."

What Has Been Happening Here?

When a teacher works this way, many things happen. Miss Peterson has been stimulating the children to react to each other. In this way they actively struggle for the justice and fair play that are so important to them. In this way they really learn what makes for justice, what makes for fair play. We have seen Ralph, for instance, learning that he has to stop talking and stick to the job at hand, as a member of this class.

Moreover, Miss Peterson has been helping each child find his place in the group. Squirming Maria has been given good active work to do, Paul has been encouraged with his painting. With this teacher's support, perhaps Teresa will lose some of her need for quarreling and fighting.

Not only has the painting served as a creative activity for the group. Through it the children have been stimulated to organize their ideas, dig for new ones, find relationships in their store of information.

And all the time they are learning what goes into the making of good human relations, child to adult, and child to child.

¶ ASSEMBLY DATE

"I tell you, I just don't know what we can do for an assembly program—and only three weeks off! I have some difficult children in here, too. I'm a little scared of what they'll do if we have a play."

Here is a situation that is familiar to many of us.

"Maybe I'll just have some music—and yet I'd really like the class to do something that would draw together our class work. Yet that little bunch of 'wild men' I have . . . ."

Isn't this a familiar feeling, too? And even more

familiar are Tom and Joe, two of the "wild men." Tom and Joe just don't care. They don't care about anything much. Mrs. Wilson, their teacher, knows they're not unintelligent boys, yet they read down around third grade level and they're eleven years old. The boys are not alike except in their "don't care" attitude. Joe seems to be the leader. Joe is a big fellow for nearly twelve. He's dressed poorly. His shirt hangs out of his pants a good deal of the time. He rarely looks at the teacher. Joe spends about half of the whole school time talking to Tom, quarreling over a lost pencil, lost paper, wandering back and forth to the pencil sharpener, to the waste basket, to the bathroom. Tom is smaller than Joe and copies Joe in every way that he can. His half-hearted attempts at working often come to nothing because of this. He was interested in the simple science experiments concerning air pressure, but Joe's inattention led him away. Mrs. Wilson is worried about these two boys, but as she says, she has other worries too, a roomful.

What Can She Do About It?

Why are Joe and Tom at such loose ends? What is making them the unhappy boys that they are? There is

no one answer to that, of course. Mrs. Wilson, through her parent conferences, has learned a little about Joe's life at home. It isn't a very happy situation, and there is little she can do about it. But she feels there must be some things she can do to help Joe right in the classroom. She reasons to herself, "What would make Joe feel better? What would push him out of this 'don't care' attitude? I'm sure that like most children of his age, Joe wants to belong . . . . If I could only find the way to make him feel he did belong here a little bit. I wonder if a play might not do it after all—a play for the assembly program."

Mrs. Wilson and her class had been working on South America and Mexico in their Social Studies. The children had learned something of Bolivar, Juarez, San Martin, Toussaint L'Ouverture. They had sung some of the interesting Brazilian songs, been interested in the bull fights. Mrs. Wilson sensed that maybe Tom and Joe would get something out of *being* some of these heroic figures in history—men like Bolivar, Juarez, Lincoln. She felt that for the boys to *identify* with these men who were brave, adventurous, and had a feeling for people and justice, would help them in their own personal problems.

The class had little difficulty deciding, in discussion with Mrs. Wilson, on the kind of play they would like to put on. It would not have to be more than a set of interrelated scenes, constructed loosely around the central idea that men like Lincoln, Juarez, Bolivar, San Martin, were all heroes, and all similar heroes in some ways.

Mrs. Wilson saw to it that active, rambunctious Joe became the active, good leader, Bolivar. And Tom? Tom must be given the chance not to follow Joe but to be on a level with him. Tom must be the Indian leader, Juarez.

Ordinarily, Mrs. Wilson encouraged the children to choose their own parts in plays, but for this class she felt that she must choose the parts, and she gave a great deal of thought to it. One of her "cops and robbers" boys was picked to play the lurking, hiding spy. Quiet, unassuming Mary was given a chance to be a regal court lady.

Joe was delighted with his part as Bolivar but he discovered when the class discussed the play that he didn't know enough about him—which meant he would have to do more reading. Mrs. Wilson had some fairly easy pamphlets and Joe really got to work. His constant "acting up" in class was being given a legitimate outlet. He could be a real actor, and that was fine!

Shaping The Play

The second time the class met to work on the play, half of them constructed scenery with paint and brown paper, while the others started the rehearsal. The lines were the children's, made up out of their Social Studies information and their imaginations, too! The play took shape as the children rehearsed. They found out what they had to say and do as they actually tried to live out their parts:

Bolivar (Joe): "I will free this country from the cruel Spanish rule! I know their ways, their cunning!"

Captain: "We have the men. Let's start!"

A child in the "audience" interrupts: "You don't have the men, you dopes! You have to ask Toussaint L'Ouverture."

Bolivar: "Oh, that's right, and he'll give me men if I promise to free the slaves."

Lincoln: "Yes, you freed the slaves in South America before we did in the United States."

Juarez (Tom): "Oh, let's go. I want to get to my scene with Lincoln."

Mrs. Wilson's help is needed here: "Let's get the order of the scenes straight at this point. Remember,

Mary, Bolivar comes to talk to you before he goes ahead with his plans. What will you do?"

"I'll refuse to have anything to do with him or his plans. I'll tell him he's a fool to think of getting away from Spanish rule!"

"All right—now we'll want the opening court scene first. What next?"

Joe remembers: "Bolivar is disgusted and talks to his captain."

"Fine, and what next?"

No answers.

"Well, how do you think the court knew anything of Bolivar's plans?"

"The spy! The spy can come in."

A Step In The Right Direction

When the spy actually did come in, on the day when the play was given before the Assembly, he almost brought down the house, simply because he was such a spy-like spy, so dramatically immersed in his part. This "cops and robbers" child really had something to say as a spy!

Joe, too, was powerful and heroic—a transformed boy, for the moment. He did not look like the same child as he strode about purposefully, his shirt well tucked in! As for Tom, it did not matter that his voice was a little weak, that he practically ran from the stage when he made his exits. He was Juarez, a leader. He had things to say to Bolivar, to Lincoln. A taste of bravery and strength and importance.

It did not matter that the play did not go entirely smoothly, that there were pauses here and there. The actors were convincing, the class had worked together as a group, and as a group had been able to produce a play for the rest of the school.

Of course Tom and Joe were not completely made over. Their success in the play did not mean that Joe would never again refuse to read, or that Tom would stop being so dependent on Joe. It did mean a step in the right direction for them, however, as well as for Mary and the others who took part, a step toward constructive achievement and acceptance in the group. With Mrs. Wilson's understanding help more steps would be taken.

¶ DICK AND THE FORTY-FIVES

As Miss Seymour took her keys out of her box, she was thinking about the discussion during Faculty Meeting the previous day. The principal had been talking about Language Arts, and had been reading to the staff some of the original stories children in the school had been writing. Miss Seymour was thinking how hard it was to get her class to write at all. Well, maybe she had been working too hard at it, worrying over it. Today she would try a new idea. Perhaps right after their gym period would be a good time.

Late Again

Around the edge of the door peered a small face. Miss Seymour looked at the face and then at the clock. It was late all right, late even for Dick.

"Well, Dick, what was it today?" she asked. Dick didn't answer, just sidled over to his seat.

"Aw, it was another fight, that's what it was!" said a yellow-haired boy in the first row. "I saw him, Miss Seymour. He had a couple of guns, too!"

"All right, Bill, that will be enough. I think that Dick can speak for himself. I'd like to know about those 'guns,' Dick."

"They're just these, Miss Seymour. Only these." Dick showed her his two toy forty-fives, digging them out of his pockets.

"Do you have to have those with you, Dick?" asked Miss Seymour.

"Well, you see, sometimes I need them—"

A great guffaw came from yellow-haired Bill in the front row.

"All right, Dick, just let me have those weapons of yours until you're ready to go home." Dick brought them slowly over to Miss Seymour.

Then she turned to the class. "Now let's get started on our writing. I thought it might be fun to try something new today, a kind of game." (Not that Dick will be able to try anything, after this, she thought to herself.)

What Happened Next?

"I'm going to write some ideas on the blackboard, some hints for stories. Just a minute, don't start writing yet, I'll show you what I mean." She wrote on the board:

As exciting as—

When she turned around to face the class, she could see that the children were all attention, eager and interested.

"Do you already have some ideas? What is the most exciting thing you can think of?"

Hands flew up all over the room.

"All right, George, you tell us."

"I think the most exciting thing would be to ride in a plane."

"No, in a rocketship," burst in Hank.

"What about as exciting as discovering another Universe?" from another child.

"Miss Seymour, Miss Seymour! I know something *much* more exciting! Exciting as slashing your way through the African jungle with the natives chasing you with their blowguns and you were unarmed . . ."

"Oh, wonderful." Miss Seymour felt almost as excited as the children. "I see that you have lots of good ideas. Let's write them down now, and I'll put some more hints on the board." She turned and wrote:

> As dark as—
> As slippery as—

And then, with Dick still in her mind she added, as though especially for him:

> As scary as—

The children bent over their desks, writing. Dick too.

When the time came for the children to read to each other what they had written, Dick was very hesitant. He didn't want to read his story, yet Miss Seymour sensed from the way he squirmed in his seat and looked around at the other children that he really did want to have a part in this. She read his story for him. He had written:

"As scary as the time the big black figure stood in ambush waiting for me. I knew he was there but I had to go by—I had to!"

The children listened intently. "Go on! Go on, Dick!" they called out. "What happened next?"

Dick looked shyly around at the class. Miss Seymour suddenly got an idea. "This could be our next step, couldn't it? Let's make these ideas into real stories. They're good enough for stories."

Child At Work

Dick plunged right to work. Miss Seymour watched him bent over his desk, hair in his eyes, writing furiously. She had never seen him work at anything so hard before.

This particular story disturbed her somewhat, but she felt that Dick was writing about something very close to him, something that he was afraid of. Just what this fear was, she did not know. But maybe this opportunity to bring it into the open might help him a bit.

One thing she knew for sure. The fact that the children had liked the beginning of his story meant a great deal to Dick. He was a boy who usually found some way to get into trouble in the class. He was often unhappily outside of things. Clay, paints, free dramatics had little appeal to him. But here was something he could do. Here was something to hang on to, an anchor for his shaky prestige.

Miss Seymour knew that Dick might have to have more help than she alone could give him, help from specialists in the school. But she also knew that he needed to have the kind of daily help that he could get in his classroom.

As she collected these first "stories" from the children, she was busy turning over in her mind some ideas for another day: As mysterious as—As sad as—As happy as—

Maybe some of these stories could go into the school newspaper—Dick's especially. Maybe some of them could provide material that the children would like to dramatize, and of course she could help the children polish up their spelling. Dick would never forget how to spell an interesting word like "ambush." She would bring poetry in to read to the class, too; ballads and other dramatic poems that would appeal to the children's feeling for excitement and adventure.

Miss Seymour felt confident now that she was on the right track, that she had discovered the way to approach creative writing with her children. It was a way that enabled the children to write about things that were really meaningful to them personally. No telling what she might be able to accomplish in this way with Dick, and with other children who needed such outlets and satisfactions.

¶ A CHINESE BOWL

"Martha! You're ten years old and you're still biting your nails! Can't you remember not to? Here's your paper with the arithmetic problems. You see they're almost all wrong. You just daydream, Martha!"

Martha stood looking down at the floor.

"Yes, Miss McAllister," she said.

"Martha, what shall I do with you? Can't you try to pay more attention? And this nail biting—it's just a bad habit."

"Yes, Miss McAllister," said Martha.

And then she walked slowly to her seat. When she sat down at her desk she looked with a worried frown off into space. Her straggly hair fell down over her forehead.

"Martha! Take your arithmetic book out and try to correct your problems. I'll try to help you in a few minutes. You must try to catch up."

Martha got out her book and began hurriedly looking for the page she wanted. When she found it, her thumb stole to her mouth, and when Miss McAllister looked up there was Martha biting away at her nails and frowning at her arithmetic paper.

It doesn't look very promising for Martha, does it? And Miss McAllister is trying very hard. She's worried about Martha and doing her best to break her of her "bad habits." But it seems that Martha doesn't ever get rid of her nailbiting or daydreaming. She merely switches from one to the other. Miss McAllister is worried about Martha's work. And look at Martha—she's worried too.

The Next Class

Martha *is* worried. Her worries are not the kind that come and go. Next term, when she moves on to Mrs. Stern's fifth grade class, she is the same Martha, face puckered into a troubled frown, nails jagged and bitten.

Arrangements have been made for her to see the social worker this year. But in the meantime, she is in the classroom, in Mrs. Stern's hands, a pupil and a member of a group of children her own age.

One day Mrs. Stern brought clay into her class. She didn't attempt to give it to all the children. In the first place, she didn't have enough; in the second place, its use required a good deal of individual attention on her part, more than she could give to the whole class at a time. So she made it very clear that the clay group would rotate, and she wrote the names of the next group on the board. A lot of difficulty was avoided in this way. It was fair. The children knew they would get a chance. Their "sense of justice" was respected.

Martha was in the first group. To her, as to the other

children, clay was a fairly new medium. They played with it, squeezed it, flattened it. Mrs. Stern let them. Martha made little round fruits, put them in a basket. She made these over and over, absorbed, working hard. Mrs. Stern had a clay period every day for a while, so that all the children got a chance to work with the clay within a week. When it came around to the first group's second chance, Mrs. Stern said to Martha:

"Would you like to try a bowl this time, Martha? You could use it for fruit or candy or anything you like."

"But I don't know how to make a big bowl like that," said Martha, beginning to turn away.

"I'll show you how easy it is. See, roll out long 'snakes.' They'll be the coils for the bowl. Then we'll pile them one above the other."

Martha looked dubious, but since Mrs. Stern stayed right with her and helped, she tried it.

"Look, Martha. Smooth the sides, now, inside and out. If you want to keep it rougher you can. Whatever you want," said Mrs. Stern as she worked along with Martha.

Then she left her and went on with her group work on the other side of the room, where some of the children were trying to use real Chinese brushes and write Chinese characters. In their study of China and its people, the calligraphy had especially intrigued them.

When Mrs. Stern glanced at the clay group every now and then, she noted that Martha's whole energy was concentrated on her work. There was no nail biting, squirming, no need for daydreaming.

What happened to that bowl was wonderful. Martha decided to make it a Chinese Bowl. She smoothed it, dried it, and painted it with poster paint a beautiful Chinese yellow, and curled a design on it with a pen nib.

"*Martha!* It's *beautiful*, and it looks like a real Chinese bowl!" the children exclaimed.

Honest admiration like this from the children; a concrete contribution to the work of the class; a learning situation that was exciting and meaningful through the opportunity it offered for creative outgo: these were the tools Mrs. Stern was working with.

Miss McAllister had been worried about Martha and rightly so. Mrs. Stern was worried too. But Mrs. Stern was concerned with finding ways and means by which Martha could see herself as an able and constructive person. From there she could go on to better things in all her work and play. Miss McAllister had not been concerned with looking for things in Martha that could be tapped and used; she tried only to verbalize and scold away the "bad habits"—with the best intentions in the world, of course.

But it is an interesting thing that a child can make his own way slowly toward achievement when he is given the right materials to work with, under the right guidance.

A handful of clay can accomplish wonders, particularly when it is presented with encouraging words, constructive help and the expectation of success.

By RUTH A. SONNEBORN:

¶ NORA, Who Clung to Her Role

Mr. Klein's hand shook a little as he looked at his wrist watch. It was really more of a tremble than a shake. He looked at the thirty-seven children sitting in rows in front of him. Most of the thirty-seven heads were bent over the desks, but here and there a child was glancing out of the window, chewing a pencil, scratching a head. Curly black heads, shiny black heads, curly yellow heads, shiny yellow heads, a red head, and browns of every shade and texture. Was there ever a more mixed population than his sixth grade this year? His "melting pot," he thought.

The period alloted to the arithmetic test was almost over. It was nearly time for social studies. He noticed his hand tremble slightly again. Why was he always nervous just when his class began to work on a play? Always? He smiled to himself. He had been teaching sixth graders for five years and last year was the first year the theme "Living and Working Together in the World" had been climaxed with a play. Mrs. Robinson, the workshop leader, had suggested it, and when the idea had both attracted and blocked him, she had offered to work with his class and help them develop a play.

"*A Loaded Word*"

He remembered how after one session, he had stopped her when the children left the room. "That was a loaded word you used today," he had said. "What word?" "Jew," he answered.

She had looked surprised. "Didn't it have to be said?" she asked. "We were talking about forced migrations of people in the world today and how Fascism has created them."

"Yes, but . . . ."

"But?"

"Shouldn't you take into account the composition of this school?"

"Every child was thinking the word," she answered. "It was best to say it."

And she had been right. The very next day the children had created a scene in the play with Nazi storm troopers which had been a wonderful and meaningful outlet for them.

The Atom Bomb Inspires A Play

Mr. Klein had always enjoyed teaching social studies. Particularly the sixth grade theme "Living and Growing Together in the World." He liked to spread before his class its limitless richness of history, geography, folklore. At the end of each year he managed to wrap up the whole program by emphasizing the special gifts of each country and race with accent on their contributions to the U.S.A. Current events had never played a part in the theme. It was always a conscientiously separate period. That is until last year when Mrs. Robinson had used the children's interest in the live news of the world, had helped them to integrate it with their social studies. The play had been the final flowering.

This year the children were obsessed as was the whole

world with the news of the atom bomb. Their interest persisted through the year. Mr. Klein had talked to Mrs. Robinson about it. He wondered whether the class could have enough understanding of the significance of the new discovery to use it in a play. Mrs. Robinson encouraged him to try. The results astounded him. The children were so excited that scenes built up and dialogue flowed so fast he could hardly jot everything down. And it was good too. Take that first scene for instance. The children had chosen to make it a street scene on the day when the news of the atom bomb had reached the newspapers in screaming headlines. It was dramatic, but more than that, it held the whole core of the play, the whole core of the year's theme. It showed the children's pride in their country and at the same time their realization that it takes many nations and peoples working together to take the big step that advances the world's knowledge.

Mr. Klein opened up his folder and satisfiedly reread the last half of the scene.

END OF SCENE I

FIRST BOY: It sure takes the Americans to do something like this. The Americans have the know-how and the how-to and all the other stuff it takes.

SECOND BOY: I read that Einstein was in on this, too.

THIRD BOY: Come to think of it, Einstein was German-born.

FIRST BOY: Gosh, I think he was kicked out of Germany by Hitler because he was a Jew.

SECOND BOY: Look at this! A scientist named Fermi worked on this. He's Italian. And he's been working right down here at Columbia University.

THIRD BOY: Hey, look! Here's a fellow from Denmark, and his name is Bohr.

FIRST BOY: And look! Here's a woman's picture in this article.

SECOND BOY: And it says she's German! Her name is Lise Meitner. I'll bet she was kicked out of Germany, too.

THIRD BOY: That's just what it says. The S.S. guards came after her and she was kicked out.

First Boy: Well, I guess we weren't the only ones that made the atom bomb.

Second Boy: Yeah, I guess it took the whole world to make the bomb.

All Except The Very Rich

It was a fine opening scene and he was proud of the class. He looked at the children again. There were few schools in New York City that represented such a rich and wide ethnic and economic community. P.S.—was within the fringe of a Negro ghetto. Besides it was a neighborhood that had attracted a large group of Jewish refugee families from Germany. It was near enough to a prosperous row of apartment houses so that some children came from middle class, middle income families. There were several blocks that housed families of low-income whites. And there was even a sprinkling of Puerto Ricans, who were just beginning to arrive by plane in the city. They were all there, all except the very rich. There were no very rich.

Almost every country in Europe that you could name had had a part in producing these children. Italy, Poland, Russia, Czechoslovakia, France, England, Ireland . . . .

Nora, Who Was Hostile

Ireland . . . his eyes found Nora, Nora with the pale blue eyes, sturdy body, and sharp little chin. Suddenly he realized that it was Nora who was making him feel tense. All the shadowy impressions of the year came to a focus. It was the way she turned her back and walked away as soon as one of the German refugee children joined a group she was in. It was the expression on her face when one of these children said something that drew admiration from the class or himself. It was the eager way she laughed when any of them twisted the order of words around in sentences that were clumsily Germanic. One child like Nora could open the door to group hostility and the play might be the thing to set her off.

But perhaps he was being over-anxious. Perhaps he was identifying too much with the refugee children. There were times when he felt that his strong feelings for them covered them like a mantle and left him uncovered, exposed. That's what happens, he thought, when one belongs to a minority race. He found himself suddenly wondering about the Negro teacher down the hall. How did she feel, for instance, in front of her mixed group when they discussed the Civil War? And did her children ever talk about the news stories that were so brutally anti-Negro? And if they did, did she feel as he did, especially protective of her own people, and especially vulnerable at the same time?

He cut off his thoughts and looked at his watch.

"All right, class. Time to turn in your papers."

There was a hubbub of voices and scraping chairs.

"Let's have the last child in each row collect the papers. When that's done, I'll tell you what we are going to do next."

Slowly the papers grew into a pile on his desk.

"All right. Now bring your chairs up front and let's get to our play."

The children came forward eagerly and crowded around him. Their enthusiasm was evident.

Working on Scene II

"The first scene went so well yesterday that I think we should move right ahead and tackle scene 2. You remember how we planned it?" Heads nodded and several hands went up. "Suppose in order to save time and since I have the notes in front of me, I outline it for you. You decided to have the next scene in Lise Meitner's laboratory in Germany. You wanted to show her working there with other scientists to find out more about the atom and how it could be split, and possibly lead to making the atom bomb. You wanted this scene to end when she had to escape from the Nazis and Germany. You planned a cast of three scientists, Dr. Meitner, Dr. Hahn, and Dr. Fortnich, one secretary and three Storm Troopers. Now then, who would like to try out for these parts?"

To his surprise Nora's hand shot up first. Until this moment she had sat unparticipating and withdrawn all during the work on the play.

"Yes, Nora?"

"Can I be Lise Meitner, Mr. Klein?"

"Sure," he answered and went on quickly to fill the other roles, determining not to try to interpret her wish but to be prepared for anything to happen.

The actors cleared a space to serve as a laboratory and moved desks up for working counters. The three scientists began to flick on and off imaginary switches, handle imaginary test tubes, and to carry on a dialogue rich in simple science phrases. After a few minutes the working quiet of the laboratory was shattered. The secretary burst in with "Dr. Meitner!"

"Please, I'm very busy."

"But it's important."

"What is it?"

"The S.S. have come to your home and office. They were looking for you. I've managed to get most of your important papers. Here they are."

"Thank you. I wonder why they're looking for me. I've noticed my mail has been held up lately."

Mr. Klein glanced at the written dialogue in his hand. He sat tensely on the edge of his chair. This he felt was the crucial moment, the moment with the "loaded word." He heard Dr. Hahn saying, "It must be because you're Jewish. Look! The Storm Troopers. You must get away. I'll help you pack."

He saw Nora, still quiet, moving from desk to desk collecting imaginary papers, and he heard her calm voice, "All right."

Dr. Hahn was helping her. "I'll stall them. Here are your papers. You must carry on our work."

Then Nora, her sharp little chin uplifted, walked quietly out of the imaginary door back to her seat. Mr. Klein felt his fist unclenching. There were loud thumps on the desk-door and three blustering S.S. men swaggered in. It was obvious the boys were enjoying this role.

S.S.: Heil Hitler! Where is Dr. Meitner?

Dr. Hahn: Oh, it's three o'clock. She's out to lunch. Any message?

S.S.: Yes, tell her to report to District 3 Police Station. Good day.

The S.S. tramped out, one of them stopped to rip an imaginary name off the imaginary door. The scene ended and the actors returned to their seats. The audience clapped spontaneously.

Mr. Klein spoke. "I think, I really think that was a fine first performance. What do you people think?"

Hands waved. There were dozens of comments about what was good and what could be better. One of the German refugee children said she thought Nora was a good Dr. Meitner because she acted so quiet and calm. And then the boys got to talking about laboratory equipment and what kinds of props they needed. The discussion raised some questions nobody could answer and several children offered to try to look for answers in the meager collection of books and pamphlets available at the time. The first thing Mr. Klein knew the period was over and there was not time to try out the scene again with another cast as they usually did.

"Tomorrow," he said, "we'll give other people a chance at these roles. Now, you've just time to get your chairs back before the lunch recess bell rings."

Nora Reveals A Strong Wish

The class moved the chairs back and as the bell rang began to get their coats out of their lockers. That is, all except Nora. Nora was searching for something in her desk. She was still searching when the last child tramped out.

"Nora," Mr. Klein said, "you're going to have to gobble your lunch on the double quick unless you get going."

Her head popped out from inside her desk and she looked quickly around the room. She came up to him and her pale blue eyes looked steadily at him. "Please, Mr. Klein, let me be Lise Meitner. I . . I . . I just want to be her."

Before he could answer her, she was snatching up her jacket and hurrying out.

Mr. Klein was astonished. This whole morning had been an astonishing one. He wondered why Nora had wanted to be Lise. He remembered her mother, a weary woman who had visited the school only once this year. She had four, or was it five, other children, and Nora was one of the undistinguished middle ones. Was this why, perhaps, she wanted to play Lise, a woman who had made a name for herself? And did this explain why she should choose to identify herself with a group she had scorned all year? Many thoughts crisscrossed his mind as he sat there. At the end he had come to only one conclusion. Nora's drive for the role was a deep-rooted and strong drive. He could not understand it but he believed it was healthy and should be gratified.

It took some doing but Mr. Klein managed to leave Nora in her role of Lise, and never once did any other child even try out for it. As the rehearsals went on he watched quietly. And he watched Nora other times, too. Was it only wishful thinking or was it true that there was less evidence of her antagonism to the refugee children? Or was it real? And if it was real, how could it be explained? He was frankly bewildered but he felt sure that her identification with the Jewish role could only be a positive step towards acceptance of her Jewish classmates. It must bring some measure of sympathy and understanding. Perhaps this was only a small step for Nora. Perhap it was a big step. But Mr. Klein felt sure she was moving in the right direction.

"My Name Is Lise"

It was just a couple of days after the actual performance of the play. The children were still glowing from the applause of the other classes and the praise of their parents. One morning the class was working at a year's review of spelling. Mr. Klein was calling each child in turn. He came to Nora.

"Now, Nora," he said, "How do . . . ."

She interrupted him, her voice quiet but firm and her pointed little chin suddenly more pointed. "My name is Lise . . . and I'm going to keep it," she said.

By LUCY SPRAGUE MITCHELL:

¶ WE'RE LIKE DETECTIVES!

The children were busy at their desks. Each child was doing his "research" for a report about the special South American nation that Mrs. Burns had assigned to him. Some children were reading articles in the encyclopedia or chapters in textbooks that Mrs. Burns had carefully selected for them. Other children were already writing, glancing now and then at a large political map that hung on the wall or at the headings for their reports which, to insure uniformity, Mrs. Burns had written on the blackboard. She had taken these headings from her favorite textbook that had been her standby for many years: political boundaries, area and population, climate, history, products and industries, imports and exports, food, clothes, shelter, art, education.

Mrs. Burns liked teaching and she liked children. Always she liked to feel that her pupils had a profitable

year with her and left her with "well-stored minds," equipped to face the future which for these sixth grade children meant a new school next year. Best of all, she liked this period. She felt thoroughly at home in this part of the new curriculum and approved of calling this gathering of information by the new name "research," and the familiar old books of information by the name of "source materials."

Troubling Questions

There were other expressions and instructions in the curriculum bulletin that troubled her. She could see that trips and painting a mural, for instance, were fun for children and might even be instructive but she couldn't quite feel that such activities belonged in a *school*. She was eager to learn new teaching methods. But when she tried to follow the new instructions, she felt awkward— as if she weren't teaching any more. She knew how to teach subject matter. But just how could she give her children "firsthand experiences?" How could she "use the environment?" What was meant by "self-expression in art?" What was her role in "free discussion?" How could she "relate science to social studies?"

At the moment, however, none of these puzzling questions troubled Mrs. Burns as she looked at her class in the quiet classroom. Though her face revealed nothing, she was saying to herself, "This is the way I like to see my class—all absorbed in books." She was confident that the reports these children wrote would be good. Not all of them, of course. But as a whole, these children were as satisfactory a sixth grade class to teach as Mrs. Burns had ever known in her long years of teaching.

"Books Are All We Do"

For these book-minded children, Mrs. Burns had planned a unit on the development of books. So, at the discussion period, she threw out a leading question: "What would we do if the school had no library?"

Alice spoke up, "It would be good if we had no library because then you wouldn't ask us to do research."

And many of the children smiled their approval. This was not the answer Mrs. Burns had expected or wanted—especially from Alice who always handed in neat reports of well-selected facts.

Mrs. Burns probed further, "Suppose we had no books at all—suppose we were living before books were printed?"

This time Jim answered, "Then there wouldn't be any use in coming to school because there wouldn't be anything to learn. Books are all we do at school." And again, though a bit hesitantly, the other children seemed to agree.

Something More Than Books

At the time, Mrs. Burns did not follow up the discussion. She was sensitive to her children and their remarks were disturbing to her. Looking back, Mrs. Burns thought these casual revealing remarks about not liking research and the implied protest in "books are all we do in school," started the change in her thinking.

She pondered over their meaning. Why didn't these bright children enjoy the research they did so docilely? She must be doing something wrong. No, she corrected her thinking, perhaps it was that these children needed something *more* than just books of information to enjoy their research. She couldn't take her children to South America! How could her children do research about a far-away country and about long-ago people, too, except through books that gave them the facts?

She reread the new curriculum bulletin with her new problem in mind. She tried to think how some of the new "activities," that she had thought of as "extras," might help in the children's research. Her first thought as a source of information other than books was the Museum. So off she went on an exploratory trip to the South American Indian exhibits in the Museum of Natural History. Here was information that you could *see*. As she looked at the pottery, the bone needles, the feather work, the drums made of gourds, she thought of the headings she had carefully prepared for the children to use in their reports—history, food, clothes, shelter, art. *Seeing* the actual things that those far-away and long-ago people had made, had used, was certainly a different kind of experience from reading about them. It was almost like being in the presence of the people themselves. Mrs. Burns felt a kind of inner excitement that comes from a new idea.

What Is Research Like?

So the class went on a trip to the Museum as a first step in gathering information through observation—not just through words. They arrived before the Museum was open. Mrs. Burns was annoyed with herself for not having planned ahead more carefully and wondered how she could hold 35 children after they had examined the few exhibits that were arranged in the room where they waited. To fill in the gap before opening time, she called the children together for a talk.

That turned out to be an important talk because of Robert's remark. Mrs. Burns reminded the group that this trip to see the Indian exhibits was a part of their research on South America. "You'll see lots of things that are very old—so old that they wouldn't have been preserved at all if they hadn't been buried." "Who buried them?" asked Jim with some skepticism. Mary said, "Perhaps nobody buried them, perhaps the people threw them away in a heap and perhaps dirt just washed down from a mountain and covered them up."

"Where did Mary get that idea?" wondered Mrs. Burns. She made a mental note to follow up Mary's remark some time by discussing erosion in the science period—perhaps she could work it into research about South America though at the moment she didn't see how. So she said, "Some Indians buried a man's most precious possessions with him when he died." "Who dug them up —way down there in South America?" This came from Jim again.

Mrs. Burns explained that archeologists went on expeditions just to dig up things that long-ago people had made and used. "That's the way they find out how those people lived and how they worked. Now when you are looking at those old things just try to imagine you have just dug them up and see what *you* can discover about how those people lived and worked." No child responded. Mrs. Burns went on a bit nervously. "For instance, perhaps you can guess from the pictures and designs on their pottery or gourds or in their stone carvings what animals and plants they used. That would tell you something important. I hope you will copy some of their designs—that's why I asked you to bring paper and pencils. If we have lots of sketches, we may be able to make some discoveries ourselves when we get back!"

Suddenly Robert spoke, his face alight with a new idea. "Why," he said, "research is just like being a detective!" So the class turned into detectives—magic word—and really, Mrs. Burns thought, a very good word for this kind of research.

Making Their Own Discoveries

From the discussions following their trip came so many questions that they had to go to the Museum again to try to find answers. In class, Jim made some paintings from sketches to hand in with his report. That led to modeling bowls and pots in clay and painting designs on them. Clay *is* messy work in a classroom, thought Mrs. Burns. But Jim seemed actually to *enjoy* getting his hands messy. Moreover, he began to paint on his own. When he brought her his painting one day, he announced triumphantly, "That's a llama carrying a load in Peru. He's turning his head and spitting because his load is too heavy!" And he acted out the spitting llama dramatically.

"Suppose you write a story about your llama," said Mrs. Burns quietly. But she didn't feel quiet inside, she felt excited. She was sensitive to a new kind of eagerness in her children to express what they had found out in some way—painting, dramatizing, modeling, even in writing.

At the time she didn't analyze just how her thinking about "learning" was changing. Later, she could put it into words, "I was beginning to find out that learning is an active performance, not just passive memory, for eleven-year-olds—perhaps it is for me too. I'm certainly learning actively now! Research even for children can be active exploring and making discoveries. Take the discovery that Alice made. She had been wondering why the Indians in Ecuador and Peru made such beautiful jars and jewelry out of silver and the Indians in Brazil didn't.

It seems strange. Alice is a well-informed girl. She had known that silver is found only in mountains. And she had known that Peru is mountainous and Brazil isn't. But she'd never put two and two together—had never related the work and the art of the Indians to the natural resources they found around them. That was a real *discovery* to Alice. Children's discoveries aren't new to the world but they *are new to the children*. And making a discovery is a satisfying, even an exciting, experience."

Let's Look It Up Together

Yet at times, Mrs. Burns almost regretted that she had abandoned the comfortable days when she thought research was confined to remembering what other people had discovered and written down in books. For in the class discussions following the children's reports, they asked questions she did not even know the answers to. She found herself saying to child after child, "We'll have to look that up and talk about it again tomorrow"—an admission she had thought no teacher should make before her children.

Mrs. Burns confessed that since the children had become detectives, she had to work harder than she ever had before just to keep up with their questions. It was even harder when they began on present-day South America. She could not take half the trips she thought of or that other teachers told her about that would make South America real to the children. And the trips were harder to arrange for and to take than trips to the Museum.

She made a list of possible trips: a banana boat unloading; the banana-ripening room at the Bronx Terminal Market; a neighborhood food store to see and perhaps buy some of the tropical foods—Brazil nuts, mangoes, avocados; the Bronx Zoo to see animals, birds and fish or even a neighborhood pet shop where she found tropical fish and birds; the Tropical Room and Cactus Room at the Botanical Gardens—the possibilities seemed endless!

The children began bringing in so many things that she had to rearrange the room to keep it looking halfway orderly. They brought so many pictures from magazines and newspapers that they started a picture file. One child went to a travel bureau and brought back a bundle of folders with pictures and maps. One folder had a map with little pictures on it—a cowboy in Argentina, coffee pickers in Brazil, a miner in Ecuador. Some had maps of railroads and airways. And these maps brought more questions.

"Why aren't there any railroads running *across* South America?"

"Why are there cowboys in Argentina and not in Brazil?"

Why? Why? Why?

Sometimes she didn't even know where to go for the answers. Even when she did, that was not enough. She had to find ways of letting the children discover some of the answers themselves. And the textbooks did not do this. The school geographies did not do this. They just reported a series of facts, seldom showing the relationships among them. Mrs. Burns was developing the habit of thinking in relationships. Alice, in her discovery, had pointed up the relationship between the kind of land that people lived in and the kind of work they did. But the geographies did not even have maps that showed where natural resources were. In these geographies most of the maps were political.

The physiographic maps that showed elevation in different colors were difficult for even these bright children to use to answer their questions. For these maps gave no images of the land with its mountains and mountain passes that explained early trails and later railroads.

They gave no image of how mountains could erode through rain and frost and wind, and how rivers could carry down bits of rock and finally build a plain.

Mrs. Burns was both excited and discouraged as she realized that these children needed a graphic relief map, and wondered how she could teach them to make one. "It's becoming more than I can handle," Mrs. Burns said to herself in the middle of the year. "I haven't the background or the tools to teach this way." Yet she felt she was beginning to understand what the new curriculum meant by giving children firsthand experience.

Thinking Is Seeing Relationships

Inside, she was becoming more and more convinced that children learn to *think* by raising questions and hunting for answers, and by expressing their discoveries in their own ways. And she came to believe that thinking is seeing relationships. That idea was a practical help to her. Source materials became sort of "raw" factual materials and research became seeing relationships among them. Her share in the children's research was to supply them with relevant source materials and help them to discover relationships that were new to them.

Yes, Mrs. Burns remembered this year as the hardest she ever lived through as a teacher. The next year was a little easier for she had accumulated some source materials and knew where to find more. And she had found out more about the way children learn, too. The climax of the next year was when her children wrote an original play with big, painted backdrops. And it all grew out of research and led to more research.

Mrs. Burns now says she wouldn't go back to the old way when the children felt that "books were all we had in school" even if she could. She says, "It keeps you on your toes—this kind of teaching—but your toes *do* get tired. It keeps you from feeling satisfied if your children are just getting along 'well enough'—keeps you wondering if they are working up to their abilities." And she adds, "You are always hunting for new opportunities for your young detectives to explore and watching how they go to work—that's really a kind of research for the teacher. She has to be something like a detective herself, doesn't she?"

¶ WHAT DOES "TEACHING CHILDREN" MEAN?

The thirty-five children and the teacher sat looking one another over. No wonder, for it was their first meeting and they were to spend many months together in this room before June came. And in June these children were to graduate from this familiar elementary school. Next year they would go to Junior High in the big High School. For this important year Miss Peary was to be their teacher. She was new to the school—nobody knew what she was like. All the children scrutinized her with curiosity tinged with a certain relief. She looked fairly young, fairly good-looking, with an easy, informal manner. They were certainly glad she was not the grim,

unsmiling kind. Yet some of the children felt an unde-
fined anxiety as they watched her; they would reserve
their judgment of her. Smiles were not enough to pre-
pare them for that unknown high school world where
the students seemed so grown up.

Plans All Made

For Miss Peary, too, this was an important year. It
was the first time she had taught a sixth grade group
and she was full of plans for them. She had been teaching
five years. She felt old in experience and modern in
thinking. It was a good feeling! In preparation for teaching a sixth grade class, she had re-read the notes that she
had taken at some lectures on the needs of children and
had made out a list headed, "The Emotional Needs of
Eleven-year-old Children." She had decided that she
would begin the year with a story-unit. The principal
had approved of her plan to have her class read stories
to the younger children but had added, "Remember,
Miss Peary, that though many in your class aren't yet
eleven, they'll be going on to high school next year. I'd
like to see your story unit tie up in some real way with
the sixth grade subjects." Miss Peary agreed outwardly
but with inner reservations. Her interest in a story-unit
was not much concerned with "old-fashioned facts."
Rather, she thought of this unit as a chance to teach
children—not subject matter—through knowing their interests, meeting their needs, and thus furthering their
development as human beings. That was her interpreta-
tion of the "new education."

As she read the roll call at this first meeting, Miss
Peary tried to size up each child in terms of her plans
for this class. They seemed an uneven group both in
maturity and in size. Grace was tall, carried herself well,
looked at Miss Peary with confident, big brown eyes and
spoke up clearly. Little Pauline looked years younger,

seemed embarrassed and squirmed in her seat when she answered the roll call. Ed had a sensitive, intellectual mature face that twitched occasionally. Frank, who had a cheerful, open little-boy face, looked uncomplicated. Miss Peary jotted down such mental notes as she read off the thirty-five names, unaware that thirty-five observant young minds were also jotting down mental notes about her.

Miss Peary had decided beforehand on a question she would ask the class that would set the informal tone she wished in her classroom and at the same time be an introduction to her story-unit. So, at discussion period, she asked in the bright voice she used for children, "Do you ever read the newspapers?"

There was a ripple almost like amusement among a group of boys. Frank's little-boy face certainly registered pride as he answered, "We don't read them. We *sell* them!"

Somehow Miss Peary felt deflated. High on her list of eleven-year-old needs that she planned to meet was "the need to feel grown-up." The inflection in the voice of this small boy who had just informed her that he and some of the other boys had a grown-up job of earning money implied that they were experienced men of the world and were to be treated as such; even, perhaps, that they knew a thing or two about life that she didn't. Miss Peary hastily changed from the subject of newspapers.

"I've been thinking," she said, "about a unit for you big sixth grade children. How would you like to read stories to the little children in the school?"

There was no ripple among the children at this remark. They sat and stared at her in silence. Miss Peary, undaunted, plunged into a glowing description of the unit, ending with how proud they should feel that the principal thought them equal to carrying such a responsibility.

She paused. Still no response from the children. Their faces were like masks. Miss Peary plunged on. "Now, we want to be democratic, don't we? So I'm going to ask for a vote. Who would like to begin the year with a story-unit?"

Ed, his sensitive face alight, raised his hand. But when he tried to speak, his hesitation amounted to a slight stammer. He finally managed to say that he "would like to read stories to kids." The other children were courteous but remained silent. Miss Peary quickly summed up the situation to herself: they were too young to know what they wanted—this was one of the times when she must decide for them. Her voice had a dulcet inflection as she turned to Grace. "I'm sure the rest of you agree with Ed. Don't you, Grace?" Grace frowned thoughtfully before she answered, "Will we have *time*, Miss Peary?" Miss Peary smiled indulgently, "We must always find time to help others, mustn't we, Grace? You'll see how I'll arrange it."

And in the next weeks, the children *did* see. Miss Peary thought of the year's work in two practically separate categories which in her mind represented "old fashioned" and "modern" ways of thinking. In the first category came the "acquisition of skills" and "subject matter" in the various areas stated in the official curriculum. To such old-fashioned work she gave a minimum amount of time and thought. In the second category came the really important work that "satisfied the children's emotional needs," built "social attitudes" and prepared them for "group living." The story-unit she regarded as such work—*that* was "teaching *children*"—that was her real job.

The children were scheduled for regular times at the school library. There Miss Peary expected them to spend their time selecting books they would like to read to kindergarten and first grade children. This suited the three "slow readers" in the class—Frank, who sold newspapers, was among them. These three also enjoyed the class discussion of these easy baby books and clamored for their turn to read them to the "kids." Ed, who read really difficult books with ease, also got satisfaction from the unit. For when he read to the young children, his eagerness to interest them made him lose his self-consciousness and his stammer.

But The Scheme Does Not Work

Nevertheless, Miss Peary was far from satisfied. Most of the children were certainly not responsive. They seemed almost to resist the unit as extra and unimportant work. Were they embarrassed at their adult role before the young children? Miss Peary redoubled her cheerful encouragement to give them self-confidence. Their reluctance did not decrease. She began to realize that for most of the children, her scheme was not working. The children remained apathetic or restless during library and discussion periods. One day she caught Grace reading a history book behind a propped up "baby book." When she told Pauline that her turn had come to read to the first grade, slow tears filled the little girl's eyes. Tears must mean timidity, for Pauline was certainly less mature than many in the class, thought Miss Peary. So she said cheerfully, "Why, Pauline, those books are easy for you to read!" "That's the trouble," said Pauline, lowering her head to hide her tears. "I'm not learning anything. And *what* will I do in high school next year?" Miss Peary, appalled, excused her from her turn at reading to the young children.

Taking Cues From The Children

How many of the children felt like Pauline? How many felt they weren't learning anything? Was being prepared for the new experience in high school an important "emotional need" for these children? If so, how could she meet this need? These were disconcerting questions that Miss Peary asked herself, but she faced them. If these children felt they needed more "regular" lessons, she would give them history, arithmetic and all the rest, she thought somewhat grimly. She reorganized her schedule and her plan. One day after she had heard Pauline asking Ed what book she should read in the library, Miss Peary began a discussion on the need of libraries in the world, in high school, in their own school. This led to a suggestion that they take the next library period to look through the books to find books they thought would help them in their own work. The children divided into groups to explore the books on the shelves. A few of the children, notably Grace and Ed, were evidently used to taking out books from a public library. But most of them were not. The three slow readers were at a loss and Miss Peary told them they could continue exploring the books for kindergarten and first grade. The atmosphere in the next discussion time changed subtly. Timid Pauline asked a question for the first time. "How can you find a book you want in the big libraries where there are so many books?" Miss

Peary answered, "Why don't we go and find out for ourselves?"

New Developments

The first class trip was to the local library. Miss Peary had spoken to one of the librarians and she was ready for the group. She showed them the big files. With her help, Ed hunted up *Legends of the United Nations*, and said shyly but without a stammer, that he thought the rest of the children would enjoy it as it told many favorite stories of people in many countries. The librarian showed them how to mark down the letter and number of this book on a card, what to do with the card, and told how someone could find that special book on the shelves and bring it to them to read in the library. She explained that if the teacher would give her a list of books they needed that were not in the school library, she would get them ready for the class to read at a special time. To Miss Peary's astonishment, the children were excited at the thought. Some of them even told her what subjects they wanted to know more about. She caught their excitement. She not only followed up this plan but she recognized that part of the children's excitement came from feeling "grown up" when they used a public library, and part of it came from the enriched content that they got from the books.

Soon came another development. Grace wondered if they couldn't make wider use of the school library. This idea led to a library unit for the class. The class drew up rules for the school library. They began examining all new books that came in. Miss Peary suggested that the children write book reviews of some of them. This in turn led to a contact with a publishing house. New books were sent to the library for the children to review. The reviews were posted on the teachers' bulletin board in the main office and also in the library for other children to read. As a part of book reviewing, the class had to review books for kindergarten and first grade children. Pauline suggested they ought to talk with the teachers of the younger groups. Then Ed thought they ought to watch the younger children at play or work to get a background for their reviews. Finally, Grace suggested that they again begin reading the books they had reviewed to the younger children.

Old Plan In A New Light

Here was Miss Peary's rejected plan. But she saw the difference. At first, it was *her* plan; now it was the *children's plan* developed from a series of experiences that had grown out of their own needs.

Had her list of "needs of eleven-year-old children" been wrong? Miss Peary read them over one week-end. No. These children *did* want to feel grown up. They did not want to be told they were "big sixth grade children" and at the same time be treated as little children. They did not want to be told it was democratic to have a vote in choosing their unit and then have the decision taken out of their hands. That was one mistake that Miss Peary felt she had made right at the start.

And what about this "old-fashioned" content that she had felt it right to ignore? Could one "teach children" and *nothing else?* After all, thought Miss Peary, how had these children come through to a responsible school job when they had rejected it when she tried to put it over on them? First through an appreciation of books in their need to be ready for high school work, and then through finding that "subject matter" was an interesting part of the world around them. At this point in her thinking Miss Peary felt both a bit humble and excited.

She began to ponder another question: what other kinds of experiences could these children have 'that would enrich the content and give them emotional satisfaction? Before the end of the year, she and the children answered this question in ways that surprised and delighted her. One of the librarians told the children that too much dampness injured the books. Immediately the children wanted to test the amount of humidity in the school library. They began science experiments in the classroom, made a barometer, studied evaporation and weather. Miss Peary and the class went on a trip to see books printed. This led to other science experiments. They made ink. They made paper.

One day Frank, who was always poring over the comic strips in the newspapers, made some animated drawings to illustrate a story for the little children who could not read even as well as he did. That started other children off on animated drawings. Then the idea of puppets struck someone. And the class put on a puppet show about the invention of printing.

Were the children building "social attitudes?" Were they learning "group living?" Yes, but not as a separate activity. Gradually, Miss Peary stopped thinking of her job as one that fell into two categories—teaching an old-fashioned curriculum of skills and subject matter, and teaching children. She had learned the meaning of an integrated program.

Looking Backward And Forward

All this was in the back of Miss Peary's mind as she looked at her children on graduation day. Were they ready for high school? Most of them were up to high school mathematics and knew how to use books as source materials. Ed and Grace were still ahead of the others in their reading and their knowledge of content. Frank was still a slow reader.

Yet she felt that just about all of them had gained during the year, each in his own individual way. Frank, for instance, had achieved another kind of maturity from his real interest—almost affection—for the little children who had listened to him read. Ed had gained in poise from his experience with them. Could she have helped these children more? She could not know.

And after all, Miss Peary thought, the tremendous and rewarding job of helping these children grow up, of educating them in the true sense of "leading them forth" was not hers alone. They would all go on to other teachers and to other experiences. There were full years ahead of them.

There were full years ahead of her too, Miss Peary knew. And she knew that she had learned from these children as much as they had learned from her. Next year from the beginning she would try to find ways to tie up subject matter and skills with the interests of all her children and try to make learning a pleasant experience for them all. *That*, thought Miss Peary, is a good preparation for high school or anything else.

The children said goodbye to Miss Peary, one by one. When Pauline's turn came she leaned forward and whispered, "I've had such a good time in this class, Miss Peary. Everyone has learned so much. I'm not afraid of high school any more." And this time it was Miss Peary who had to struggle not to have the tears rise.

By CLAUDIA LEWIS
and DOROTHY STALL:

Epilogue

Worth a Lifetime of Striving

We have said that a teacher who adopts certain attitudes toward her children can find her way through her maze of problems without too much difficulty.

What are these attitudes? Can they be reduced to a few simple statements, contained within one paragraph?

Perhaps they can. Let's see if we can narrow them down and arrive at the crux.

To begin with, let us formulate one rather obvious principle: When a child gives us trouble, it is probably because he is after something he needs but does not have. Our first step, then, is always to ask, "*Why* is this child doing this thing? What is he trying to gain by it? What need does it seem to fill?"

"Why?" should be the teacher's fundamental question for herself. This is her keystone. And she will be helped in answering it if she remembers two things: first, that the child in front of her has a life outside of the classroom, which she should learn something about; and second, that his needs are for happy and successful living, as well as for acquaintance with the world's accumulated store of facts and skills.

"Happy"—that is an excellent word for us to fasten upon, as we try still further to narrow down and define the teaching attitude that leads to successful solutions of classroom problems.

Children blossom and bloom and thrive in a happy atmosphere. The cheerful, buoyant teacher who has a light touch and a sense of fun is apt to be the one with the fewest discipline problems. Children are so ready to respond to affection and fun.

Are we saying, in the long run, that successful teaching is a matter of the teacher's *personality?* Everyone knows there is a certain amount of truth in this assumption. But what is "personality"? Why does there so often seem to be a distinct separation between a teacher's aloof classroom personality and the warm human personality she shows her friends when she steps out of the school building?

Granted that she is an emotionally stable person with an ordered inner life of her own, why does she not simply be herself with her children, and show them that she is a sympathetic, natural human being?

For here we have arrived at the real crux, to be contained within a paragraph. A teacher whose fundamental feeling for her children is a warm and sympathetic one, and who is quite willing to show this feeling, does not have to strain herself to figure out how she should uphold her authority, or how she should follow the best educational procedure down to the letter when classroom problems arise. She probably doesn't go far wrong if she simply sits down with the children, eye to eye, and as one human being with another attempts to figure out the difficulty, letting the children see her feeling, acting, talking, like a warm and sympathetic person.

In the foregoing sketches teachers and children are

living together in school, learning and growing together, planning and working things out together.

The better the conditions and the more abundant the materials, the less the teacher has to struggle to create a constructive atmosphere, and the more she can allow for personal initiative and encourage the natural gifts of each child.

The creative teacher is never the "perfect" teacher. She is never the teacher who knows all the answers. But this does not mean that she has no standards. She has very high standards, but they are thought of in terms of human development. Her primary interest is in personality, her belief is in life, and in the possibility of happiness for all individuals and groups.

There are always pictures in her mind of what lies beyond, of what could be—if . . . .

Next to the parents, she is closest to the child—she is most interested in helping him fulfill himself.

She moves about for a year in a little society, offering leadership here, staying in the background there, following the ebb and flow of changing friendships, shifting group loyalties. She follows the growth of self-reliance and thoughtfulness for others. She watches facial expressions change in pride, discouragement, strength, anger, gaiety, satisfaction. She sees children brooding over knotty problems, or their eyes sparkling with newly discovered knowledge and joy.

The creative teacher knows that when social and material conditions are right, the child is helped to grow into what he is meant to be. She knows what the right conditions are, and it is partly her job to help parents and administrators remove obstacles which are in the way. The obstacles are many and great, and she may never see the full fruits of her work. Yet the ideal—full human development for children, for herself, for society —is worth a lifetime of striving.

About the Authors

LUCY SPRAGUE MITCHELL
has been a leader in education ever since 1908 when she became Dean of Women, the first woman on the faculty of the University of California. She has taught all the nursery and elementary ages, and served as educational advisor to many experimental schools. For thirty-seven years she has been active at the Bank Street College of Education which she helped to found in 1916. Her books include such well known works as *The Here and Now Story Book* (Dutton), *Our Children and Our Schools* (Simon & Schuster), *Two Lives, The Story of Wesley Clair Mitchell and Myself* (Simon & Schuster), and many articles in professional and popular magazines. She is currently Chairman of the Board of Trustees of Bank Street College and is active in the publications program of the college. Her contribution to this book grew out of her participation in the planning and work of the Public School Workshops.

CLAUDIA LEWIS
received a bachelor's degree from Reed College and a master's degree in child development from the University of Minnesota. She was a founder, and a director of the Highlander Folk School Nursery in Monteagle, Tennessee for a number of years. She has been on the faculty of the Bank Street College of Education since 1943 and active in

187

the Public School Workshops. At present, as well as teaching in the college, she serves as student advisor. She is the author of *Children of the Cumberland* (Columbia University Press) and her new book *Stories in the Making,* about writing for children, will be published by Simon & Schuster in the spring of 1954.

VIRGINIA SCHONBORG

received her A.B. at Smith College and then went on to study at the Bank Street College of Education. After teaching a few years in private schools, she became assistant to the Director of the All-Day Neighborhood Schools of the Board of Education of New York City. She was an active staff member of the Bank Street Public School Workshops. At present she acts as teacher-librarian at the college and gives a course on Environment and Curriculum. She is also teaching at the Reece School in New York City.

RUTH A. SONNEBORN

graduated from the Ethical Culture Normal School and after a brief teaching experience went into advertising. As a parent of two children attending the nursery school in the Bank Street College of Education and subsequently other experimental schools, her interest in education revived. She became an active working parent in these schools and also helped organize child care courses under the program of the Civilian Defense Volunteers office. She is currently Assistant Director of Publications at the Bank Street College.

DOROTHY STALL

studied at the Kansas State Teachers College of Emporia, Teachers College, Columbia University, the New School for Social Research and the Bank Street College of Education. The study of Indian culture has been one of her major interests. She is the author of *Chuckchi Hunter* (Morrow). She has taught in public and private schools, and was formerly a member of the Public School Workshops of Bank Street College. She is now teaching at Burgundy Farms Country Day School, Alexandria, Virginia.